stress

Love
Mom.

Spirituality

THAT

MAKES

Sense

Spirituality
THAT
MAKES
Sense

DOUGLAS TAYLOR

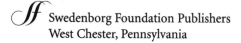 Swedenborg Foundation Publishers
West Chester, Pennsylvania

I dedicate this book to my wife, Christine—
my greatest supporter and encourager, and my
kindest and most insightful critic.

©2000 by Douglas Taylor

Library of Congress Cataloging-in-Publication Data
        Taylor, Douglas, 1925–
                Spirituality that makes sense / Douglas Taylor.
                        p.   cm.
                Includes bibliographical references.
                ISBN 0–87785–395–9
                1. Swedenborg, Emanuel, 1688–1772.   I. Title

        BX8748.T39 2000
        230'.94—dc21   99–089142

Edited by Betty Christiansen
Designed by Sans Serif, Inc., Saline, Michigan
Set in Avenir and Minion by Sans Serif, Inc.

Printed in the United States of America

For more information on Swedenborg Foundation Publishers, contact:
        Swedenborg Foundation
        320 North Church Street
        West Chester, PA 19380
                or
        http://www.swedenborg.com

CONTENTS

ACKNOWLEDGMENTS

I would like to thank members of Inquirers' Classes who have, over the years, urged me to publish the text of the classes in book form.

The support and encouragement of Mrs. Vee Nickel and Mrs. Rachel Klippenstein, who live out of state and carefully read an early draft of the manuscript, were much appreciated. Others who read the manuscript and made valuable comments were Mrs. Ralph Wetzel and the Reverend Dr. Reuben Bell.

I also want to thank the readers at the Swedenborg Foundation and the Foundation's Publication Committee who recommended publication. The editors—Susan Poole and Betty Christiansen—deserve my greatest thanks for their hours of editing and sustained interest in the project, as do the proof readers, Mr. and Mrs. Kenneth Rose.

Finally, I would like to express my gratitude to the Swedenborg Foundation for allowing me to capitalize pronouns and adjectives referring to the Lord, although this does not conform to their house style.

Douglas Taylor
Bryn Athyn, Pennsylvania

INTRODUCTION

Many people today are looking for a religion that explains things, making it possible to believe with one's eyes open, a religion that gives faith through understanding. They want to go beyond the "mysteries of faith." They want to be able to say, on hearing a religious teaching, "That makes sense. It is easy to believe that."

That is why this book is being offered. The hope is that many readers will find something that they are looking for.

I first began "looking for something" while teaching French and English in a private boys' school that was interested not only in good examination results but especially in character development. The emphasis was on Christian morality, which I admired and accepted. But, rightly or wrongly, in my experience, the doctrines taught in Christian churches seemed inadequate, raising more questions than they answered.

Yet Christian morality, deprived of its theological underpinning, was barren. It was like a tree whose roots had died. Relying on mere morality, asking whether this or that was fair or unfair, was not sufficiently appealing to adolescent youths. Something more was needed, but I did not know at the time what that something might be. Looking back now, I realize that I must have been subconsciously searching for a religious philosophy.

The spirituality I craved was provided by reading the Theological Writings of Emanuel Swedenborg, the eighteenth-century scientist, philosopher, and theologian. This satisfying experience eventually led to a strong desire to share Swedenborg with others, especially with those who were hungering and thirsting after righteousness. On becoming a pastor, it was not long before I began to give classes for inquirers. These "Inquirers' Classes" have continued for some thirty years.

"Inquirers' Classes," as the name implies, are for people with inquiring minds who would like to find a system of belief and life that takes traditional Christianity a step or two further. In effect, the classes were an introduction to Swedenborg.

The members of the classes came from several sources: friends or spouses of members of the Church; readers who had found Swedenborg's books in public libraries; people who had responded to newspaper or radio advertisements; "walk-ins" at church who wanted to know more.

The present work is the text of those "Inquirers' Classes." In the early chapters, there is a constant appeal to Scripture teaching, with quotations from Swedenborg used sparingly. Later there is increasing use of such quotations, which are really elaborations of general Bible teachings and their implications.

Part I presents an overview of a broader and deeper view of Christianity, based on what Swedenborg calls the "universal form of the Faith of the New Church." This part deals with the Lord and His work of redemption, which is "universal" because it enters into everything of life and spirituality.

Part II enters into "the particulars of faith on man's part," as Swedenborg calls them, relating theology to our daily life.

This "Faith of the New Church" is to be found in the introductory passages of *True Christian Religion,* published by Swedenborg in 1770, just two years before his death. Swedenborg there sets out the doctrine itself in systematic form. *True Christian Religion* is really a compendium of the whole theological system.

Who was Emanuel Swedenborg?

Emanuel Swedenborg was born as Emanuel Svedberg in Stockholm, Sweden, on January 29, 1688, the third child and second son of Dean Jesper Svedberg and his gracious wife, Sarah Behm. Swedenborg's father was first regimental chaplain to the king, then a professor of theology and later a bishop in the Swedish Lutheran Church. When he was ennobled by the new queen in 1719, the family name was changed to Swedenborg.

Swedenborg's interest in science was aroused by his brother-in-law, Erik Benzelius, librarian at the University of Uppsala and a keen student of mathematics and science.

After completing his university studies in philosophy at the age of twenty, Swedenborg went on a foreign journey to complete his education. In London, he lodged with various tradespeople, learning their arts and crafts. He studied the works of Newton, introducing them into Sweden; he studied mathematics at Oxford, and conferred at length with the astronomers Flamsteed and Halley. In general, he took every opportunity to meet the world's best thinkers of his day. Looking back on this period in his old age, he recognized it as the beginning of his preparation for his life's work.

After two-and-a-half years in England, Swedenborg visited Holland, France, and Germany. At this time, he listed plans for fourteen mechanical inventions, including:

> The plan of a certain ship which, with its men, can go under the surface of the sea, wherever it chooses, and do great damage to the fleet of the enemy.

> A universal musical instrument, by means of which one who is quite unacquainted with music may execute all kinds of airs, that are marked on paper by notes.

> A flying carriage, or the possibility of remaining suspended in the air, and of being conveyed through it.

> A method of ascertaining the desires and affections of the mind by analysis.

On his return to Sweden after an absence of five years, Swedenborg collaborated with Christopher Polhem, the great Swedish inventor, publishing at his own expense what is now recognized by the Swedish Royal Academy of Science as its first scientific periodical. He also worked for twenty-five years as a superintendent of mining in Sweden.

This kept him in touch with the work-a-day world, but he was also active in the learned world. He was a pioneer in geology, and wrote the first Swedish textbook on algebra. In addition, he managed to acquire a European reputation as a front-rank philosopher. From his pen there flowed the following major works in philosophy: *Philosophical and Mineralogical Works; The Principia, or First Principles of Natural Things; The Infinite and Final Cause of Creation; The Economy of the Animal Kingdom* (the body being the kingdom of the soul or *Anima;* and *The Animal Kingdom,* a sequel.

As the titles of the last two works on anatomy indicate, Swedenborg had become increasingly interested in the soul, specifically in a question that intrigued eighteenth-century philosophers: where is the seat or dwelling place of the soul?

In *The Animal Kingdom* (published in 1744–1745), Swedenborg realized that he had reached the threshold of the soul. He had gone as far as reasoning from the scientific method could take him.

This realization led to the turning point of his life, his transition from being a philosopher to a theologian. He had always been a Christian philosopher, deploring the secret atheistic materialism that he encountered among a number of his scientific colleagues. His philosophic works were all designed to show that there is a realm of reality above the merely physical.

As a scientific writer who had a profound interest in matters of the spirit and sought to explain them, Swedenborg offers considerable satisfaction for spiritual seekers today.

PART

One

1

AN OVERVIEW

On the idea of God and the idea of redemption . . . every-thing of the church depends.

Emanuel Swedenborg
True Christian Religion 133[1]

Whatever our ideas on the subjects of God and redemption might be, they are without doubt the two most important ideas in our heads. These ideas enter into every aspect of theology and life. If they are distorted, our concepts of theology and religion are distorted. If they become merely natural ideas rather than spiritual,

---

[1] Emanuel Swedenborg, *True Christian Religion*, vol. 1, trans. John C. Ager, 2nd edition (West Chester, Penna.: The Swedenborg Foundation, 1996).

Throughout this book, quotations from the works of Emanuel Swedenborg are taken from the Standard Edition of the Writings of Emanuel Swedenborg (New York: The Swedenborg Foundation, 1949–1956), and will be cited within the text. Any emphasis in a quotation is the addition of the author.

As is customary in Swedenborgian studies, the numbers following titles refer to paragraph or section numbers, which are uniform in all editions, rather than to page numbers.

then our concepts of theology and religion become merely natural as well.

The Idea of God

Can anyone think of an idea that is higher or more important than the idea of God? Surely, there is no loftier idea possible for the human mind to grasp. The idea of God is not just an academic matter—an idea intended only for theologians and for dry-as-dust theorizing. Our idea of God governs and controls all our wishing and thinking, whether we realize it or not. Even atheists' ideas of God as a nonentity enter into all of their thoughts and influence their feelings and their lives—much more than they realize.

For instance, the first and great commandment is that we should love the Lord with all our heart, soul, mind, and strength (Deuteronomy 6:5; Mark 12:30). But who is the Lord? We must at the very least know about Him in order to love Him.

In our daily living, we are not to do evil for the sole reason that it is a sin against the Lord. But, again, who is the Lord? Is it Jehovah of the Old Testament or Jesus of the New Testament? Are they the same Divine Person? Whose commandments are we to obey, those of Jehovah or those of Jesus? Are they the same commandments? In order to live the life of religion, we need a clear idea of God.

The idea of God is at the center of our minds. It is also at the center of the doctrine of any church. A church that has a vague or mistaken idea of God at its center cannot hope to have clear and trustworthy ideas out at its circumference. These ideas will be at least as vague out there as they are at the center.

For instance, if we are taught that there are three persons in God, each of whom is God, yet that there are not three gods but one God, then even very thoughtful and highly intelligent people will find this idea quite incomprehensible.

But how can such a vitally essential idea be incomprehensible? How can the most noble and important idea that there is be impossible to grasp—a *mystery?* If God is *completely* beyond our comprehension, then He is invisible to the human mind. This should give us pause. It should make us wonder whether the idea of God as being an unfathomable mystery is really not a *mys*tery, but perhaps a *mis*take.

To think of God as invisible to the human mind means that we have a blind faith in God. We cannot *see* Him. This reminds us of the Lord's condemnation of the leaders of the Jewish Church as "blind leaders of the blind" (Matthew 15:14), and of His complaint to the Samaritans: "You worship what you do not know; we know what we worship" (John 4:22).[2]

It is true that the finite human mind can never fully comprehend the Infinite. We would indeed require an infinite, Divine intellect to have a complete understanding of the Infinite. But that truth is too often abused, stretched to the point of stifling discussion before it has scarcely begun. It is possible to go further and develop a much clearer idea of God and of redemption. A vague idea of God has unfortunate consequences.

The first consequence is that people, sooner or later, begin to think that the idea of God is not important. If we are urged not to worry about the difficulty of understanding God, not to trouble ourselves with the mystery but to get on with doing what God says in His commandments, then we are choosing between understanding and doing, rather than choosing to do *and* understand as well.

There is no doubt that we should follow the Lord's commandments. There is no question about that. But the effect of believing that our idea of God is of no great consequence is quite devastating to our spiritual life and, consequently, to the life of the

---

[2] All quotations from the Bible used in this book, unless otherwise noted, are taken from the New King James Version (Nashville, Tenn.: Thomas Nelson Publishers, 1982), and are used by permission of the publisher. Any emphasis used in a quotation is an addition of the author.

church. It results in people's thinking about God less, in having less faith in Him, and finally in coming to leave God out of their lives altogether. While they may, indeed, continue to obey His Ten Commandments and His teachings in the New Testament for a few generations, they will progressively put less and less emphasis on them as *Divine* commandments. They will gradually come to regard them as rules and regulations, not immutable laws. A law is not like a rule or regulation, such as a highway code, which may sometimes be broken with impunity. Not so a law. A law is a description of the way a thing operates. One cannot break the laws of the physical universe without incurring some penalty. If we defy the law of gravity, for instance, we come to grief. It is the same with all laws on the physical plane, and on the spiritual plane as well.

On the other hand, we can break rules and "get away with it"; therefore, people who think of the Lord's commandments as nothing more than rules will develop schemes for getting around them. Finally, they will look on these Divine teachings as merely human teachings. When that point has been reached, people may indeed be doing good, ethical, moral acts—good in the sense that they have a beneficial effect on other people. But in themselves, in their origins, these works will not be good. There will be no Divine motivation for them. They will not go forth from a good root but a bad one. Can a rotten tree bring forth good fruit? (See Matthew 7:17–18.) A deed is only as good as the motive from which it springs.

The idea of God is therefore full of practical implications.

The Idea of Redemption

The ideas of redemption and salvation are similar. In popular language, *to redeem* means "to buy back by paying a stipulated price" (Webster's International Dictionary). Theologically, it refers to the whole purpose of the Lord's coming, the process by which the Lord bought back or redeemed the human race from every kind of destruction, and the price He paid in achieving that. Salvation refers to a *particular* redemption—the saving or rescue of an individual person from a life of hell (here and hereafter)—not simply from the punishment inherent in evil, but from sinning itself.

But if we are saved from the punishments of hell simply by believing that the Lord Jesus Christ took all the punishment for us on the cross—that it is our belief *alone* that saves us—then there will not be much emphasis on doing what is good from a religious or spiritual motive. Self-examination and shunning evils as sins will also seem unnecessary. Faith or belief will be the central focus as far as salvation is concerned. I have even heard it said by a preacher that "we should live a moral life, but it has nothing to do with our salvation." Once again, the life of religion and the life of the church will be gradually devastated, becoming merely natural.

The idea of God and the idea of redemption are matters of great practical importance, and of *supreme* importance. These ideas have a series of consequences into eternity.

Swedenborg presents some penetrating ideas about God and redemption. He calls them "the faith of the New Church," and in *True Christian Religion* 2, he summarizes them in these words:

> The Lord from eternity who is Jehovah, came into the world to subjugate the hells and to glorify His Human; and without this no mortal could have been saved; and those are saved who believe in Him.

That statement is a mixture of unfamiliar New Church terminology and familiar Christian terms. Any reader with even a rudimentary Sunday School introduction to the Christian religion will easily recognize such words as *the Lord, eternity, Jehovah, the hells, saved,* and especially *those are saved who believe in Him.*

This familiarity with certain terms may lead to the conclusion that there is nothing very new in this statement. Surely, we have all heard about God incarnate coming into the world to save us, and only those are saved who believe in Him. But a closer look at this passage reveals some quite marked differences from familiar ideas; for example, it is *Jehovah* who came into the world, that His purpose was "to subjugate the hells" and to "glorify His Human." These differences are the reason Swedenborg calls this the faith of the "*New* Church." They take Christianity a step or two further.

Having discussed the New Church faith in its universal form, which tells us about God's part, we will then turn in Part II to the particulars of this faith with reference to our part, which are set forth in the next article in *True Christian Religion* 3:2, as follows:

1. God is one, in whom is a Divine trinity, and the Lord God the Savior Jesus Christ is that one.

2. Saving faith is to believe in *Him*.

3. Evils should not be done, because they belong to the devil and are from the devil.

4. Goods should be done, because they belong to God and are from God.

5. These things should be done by man as if from himself; but it should be believed that they are done from the Lord in man and by means of man.

The first two are matters of faith, the next two of charity, and the fifth (a matter) of the conjunction of charity and faith, thus of the conjunction of the Lord and man.

2

THE CREATOR
AS THE REDEEMER

The Lord from eternity, who is Jehovah, came into the world.

Emanuel Swedenborg
True Christian Religion 2

The above statement indicates that Jehovah the Creator Himself came into the world to be the Redeemer. In other words, it tells us that Jesus is Jehovah in human form.

That conclusion is quite startling to anyone who has accepted uncritically the doctrine that the Bible distinguishes between the Father, who has never come on earth, and the Son, who did come. Yet the Scriptures show that the Divine Being who came into the world in a physical form, by means of birth through the virgin Mary, was actually the Creator, the *only* Divine Person—God Himself. The Creator became the Redeemer.

Isaiah 9:6 says: "For unto us a Child is born, unto us a Son is given; and the government will be upon His shoulder. And His name will be called Wonderful, Counselor, Mighty God, Everlasting Father, Prince of Peace." He who is called the Son is also called the Father: "Mighty God"—not a mighty god, but Mighty God. Since the "Everlasting Father" is Jehovah, and "a Son" is Jesus, Jehovah and Jesus must be one and the same Divine Person.

This passage is not the only one that makes this identification. In fact, *all* the passages in the Old Testament about the coming of the Lord say that it is *Jehovah* who will come. The most explicit is in Psalm 18:9: "The LORD [Jehovah] bowed the heavens also and came down." But there are others:

> And it will be said in that day: "Behold, this is our God; we have waited for Him, and He will save us. This is the LORD [Jehovah]. . . . We will be glad and rejoice in His salvation." (Isaiah 25:9)

> The voice of one crying in the wilderness: "Prepare the way of the LORD [Jehovah], make straight in the desert a highway for our God. . . . Behold, the Lord God shall come with a strong hand." (Isaiah 40:3, 10)

> "Behold, the virgin shall conceive and bear a Son, and shall call His name Immanuel [God with us]." (Isaiah 7:14)

Only One God

Besides this, the Old Testament also repeatedly says that there is, was, and always will be only one God:

> "I am the LORD [Jehovah] and there is none else. There is no God beside Me." (Isaiah 45:5)

> "Before Me there was no God formed, neither shall there be after Me. I, even I, am the LORD [Jehovah]: and beside Me there is no Savior." (Isaiah 43:10–11)

> "Who has told it from that time? Have not I the LORD [Jehovah] ? And there is no other God beside Me; a just God and a Savior;

there is none besides Me. Look to Me and be saved, all you ends of the earth: for I am God, and there is no other." (Isaiah 45:21–22; see also 42:8; 44:6; 48:11)

The name *Jehovah* is what is said in the original language. The King James translators, however, knowing that Jewish readers regard the name *Jehovah* as too holy to utter and usually prefer the name *Adonai* (the Lord), substituted instead the name *LORD*, spelled in capital letters, not lowercase, as with *Adonai*. The New King James does the same. So, whenever we find the name *LORD* in capital letters, we are to understand that the name *Jehovah* is used in the original. This is the name used in the above quotations. It brings out even more clearly the Old Testament truth that there is but one God in one Person.

If this is indeed the teaching of the Old Testament, the same idea should surely be confirmed in the New Testament. We find that this is, in fact, the case, as we read in the beginning of the Gospel of John:

> Everything was made by Him; and not one thing that was made was made without Him . . . . He was in the world, and He made the world, and the world did not know Him. (John 1:3, 10, The Good News Bible).

There are many other places in the New Testament, especially in the Gospel of John, where it is clearly taught that Jesus is Divine, many of them in the words of the Lord Himself:

> [Jesus said]: "I and the Father are one." (John 10:30)

> He who has seen Me has seen the Father; so how can you say, "Show us the Father?" (John 14:9)

> Before Abraham was, I AM. (John 8:58)

I AM can have but one meaning; it is Jehovah's name (Exodus 3:14), the Divine Being.

Even Thomas the doubter called Jesus, "My Lord and my God!" (John 20:28). Later, Jesus told the disciples, "All authority is given to Me in heaven and on earth" (Matthew 28:18), and in the Book of Revelation He calls Himself "the Almighty" (Revelation 1:18).

So the Scriptures present two important truths: (1) that there is but one God in one Person; (2) that Jesus is Divine. There is only one way of combining these two truths; they lead unavoidably to the conclusion that Jesus is that one God, that He is the one God of the Old Testament (Jehovah) in human form. In other words, before He came on earth, God was called Jehovah, but after He came on earth, He was known as Jesus. In this connection, it is interesting to know that the name *Jesus* is from the Greek form of the Hebrew name *Jehoshua*, which means "Jehovah saves."

The teachings about the Savior and the "First and the Last" give further evidence. With regard to the Savior, two of the quotations already brought forward from the prophet Isaiah said that Jehovah is the *only* Savior:

I, even I, am Jehovah: and beside Me there is no Savior. (Isaiah 43:11)

Who has declared this from ancient time? Have not I, Jehovah? And there is no other God beside Me; a just God and a Savior; there is none beside Me. Look to Me and be saved, all the ends of the earth: for I am God, and there is none else. (Isaiah 45:21–22)

There are also several other examples:

All flesh shall know that I, Jehovah, am your Savior and your Redeemer, the Mighty One of Jacob. (Isaiah 49:26; see also 60:16)

Thus says Jehovah, your Redeemer . . . who makes all things, who stretches forth the heavens alone, who spreads abroad the earth by Myself. (Isaiah 44:24)

I am Jehovah your God ever since the land of Egypt, and you shall know no God but Me; for there is no Savior beside Me. (Hosea 13:4)

Yet if we were to ask most churchgoers in the Christian world, "Who is the Savior?" the reply would undoubtedly be Jesus, because of the many passages in the New Testament in which Jesus is called the Savior:

And she shall bring forth a Son, and you shall call His name Jesus: for He shall save His people from their sins. (Matthew 1:21)

For to you is born this day in the city of David a Savior, who is Christ the Lord. (Luke 2:11)

And [the men] said to the woman, Now we believe, not because of your saying: for we have heard Him ourselves, and know that this is indeed the Christ, the Savior of the world. (John 4:42)

The writings of the early Christian Church also called the Lord Jesus Christ the Savior. To give but one example:

Looking for that blessed hope and glorious appearing of our great God and Savior, Jesus Christ. (Titus 2:13)

So Jehovah says He is the *only* Savior and Redeemer, but in the New Testament, Jesus is called the Savior. It must be the same Divine Person who is spoken of. Jesus is Jehovah on earth in His own human form. The Creator came in order to be the Savior and Redeemer.

With regard to the passages on "the First and the Last," we see something similar. Both Jehovah in the Old Testament and Jesus in the New claim to be the First and the Last. But it is impossible to have two in the position of either the first or the last. So, again, it must be the same and the only Divine Person who is the First and the Last.

Jehovah calls Himself the First and the Last in the following passages:

I [Jehovah] am the First, and I am the Last. (Isaiah 44:6)

I [Jehovah of hosts] am the First, I also am the Last. (Isaiah 48:12)

But Jesus calls Himself the First and the Last as well. Note that alpha and omega are the first and the last letters of the Greek alphabet:

I am Alpha and Omega, the Beginning and the End, the First and the Last. (Revelation 22:13)

I am Alpha and Omega, the Beginning and the End, says the Lord, who is, and who was, and who is to come, the Almighty. (Revelation 1:8)

Both the Old and New Testaments say that it was the Creator who came into the world, and that consequently the Father and the Son are not two but *one* Person. "The Lord from eternity, who is Jehovah, came into the world" (*True Christian Religion* 2).

But what does this do to the traditional doctrine of the Trinity? How are we to understand those passages, especially in the New Testament, where the Son seems to be a Person separate from the Father? These passages have to be considered. They cannot be ignored—ανψ μορε τηαν τηε πασσαγεσ ωε ηαῶε βεεν θυοτινγ χαν βε ιγνορεδ—if we wish to gain the *whole* truth about the God we are to worship. We will see in Chapter 6, on the subject of the Trinity, how these latter passages fall into place when they are seen in the light of the passages we have been examining, those that teach that there is but one God in one Person.

The question of *how* the one God was able to appear in a human form in this world leads us to the subject of the virgin birth.

The Virgin Birth[1]

Mary was the first to wonder about the possibility of the virgin birth. In response to the angel Gabriel's announcement of the forthcoming birth of the Lord by means of her, Mary said to the angel, "How shall this be, since I do not know a man?" (Luke 1:34). Yet, before the angel left her, she had not only accepted the Divinely given promise, but had also indicated clearly her complete willingness to serve the Lord, saying: "Behold the handmaid of the Lord! Let it be to me according to your word" (Luke 1:38). In the same way, Joseph, who certainly had a greater interest in this matter than anyone else, also was convinced by the message of the angel of the Lord that Mary had conceived by the Holy Spirit (Matthew 1:20) and that, consequently, she had done nothing dishonorable, but rather was highly favored.

Joseph and Mary had to be convinced, not by any means of their own, not by their own reasoning, but by supernatural means—by a Divine message faithfully delivered. It is always "the Divine that bears witness concerning the Divine, and not man from himself" (*Apocalypse Explained* 635:2). As the Lord on earth said to Simon Peter after he had declared His Divinity, "Flesh and blood has not revealed it to you, but My Father who is in heaven" (Matthew 16:17).

So must it be with all who have followed Mary in wondering how there could be a virgin birth. We cannot be convinced of it through any reasoning of our own; we can acknowledge it from the heart only as our heart is made new from above. Only from the Divine can we bear witness to the Divine. Only through what flows into us from the Lord above can we, in heart, believe in the virgin birth. Yet this belief is fundamental to Christianity.

---

[1]In this section I am greatly indebted to a sermon by the Rt. Reverend Alfred Acton, entitled "The Glorification" (*New Church Life*, December 1901, pages 639–647).

What beclouds the understanding of the natural mind when asked to consider this matter is the thought that all the miracles recounted in the Word are an intellectual embarrassment. The natural mind in us and around us is rather inclined to be impressed with its own intelligence and finds it somewhat humiliating to be told about a miracle, which, by definition, is something inexplicable, something that cannot easily be understood, something that seems to be a departure from the order of the universe—the order discovered by natural means, by scientific investigation.

However, as a general principle, what are commonly called miracles are never really departures from the Divine order, despite appearances to the contrary. If the Creator were to depart from the order that He has imposed upon His universe, He would be departing from Himself. He would be going outside of Himself because He is order and wisdom itself, in its very essence. Surely we can see the absurdity of saying that the greatest way the Lord shows His Divine order is by making some departure from it! The Lord does not set aside His laws of order at any time. What seems like a miracle to us in our ignorance is simply the Lord's introducing another law that we have not yet understood. This applies even in the matter of the virgin birth.

The greatest help in understanding the miracles of the Word is the teaching about the law of *influx*, or the way the Lord operates first in the spiritual world (the world of causes) and then in the natural world (the world of effects). Influx is the action of what is higher upon what is lower. For example, the feelings of friendship in our mind act upon our facial muscles to produce what we call a smile. The feelings are higher, the smile on the face is lower.

The term *influx* is derived from the same Latin root as the common word *influence*. To the extent that our understanding of influx, or the Divine influence, is lacking or deficient, to that extent we are baffled by the miracles of the Old and New Testaments. The world at large generally lacks a realization that the Lord our Heavenly Father is the *real* agent in any conception and birth that occurs.

Failing to see the Lord's part in human birth, the natural mind can hardly be expected to see the truth of the completely Divine conception involved in the virgin birth.

The birth of any baby is a miracle, in a certain sense. How can we believe that the seed of the father, received in the womb of the mother and fertilizing the ovum, can produce a perfect human form, complete in all its parts and fitted for life not only in this physical world but also in the eternal spiritual world? How can we possibly believe this miracle? Has any intellectually honest person at any time ever claimed to understand this process fully in all its details? How then can *we* possibly be asked to believe it?

Yet we must, because we see this happening all the time. No one can deny the *fact* of this miracle. Incontestably, it does happen, though there are some things in the process that are not fully understood by science. Scientists frankly admit that they do not know what directs the growth of the babe in the womb. What force directs the cell division so that the human form and shape result? Surely, this is a miracle, a marvel, a matter of wonder!

No light can be shed on this miracle of human birth until we human beings admit that we do not have life in ourselves, that life *flows* into us. We *receive* life; we are only receivers or recipients of life from the Lord, who alone is life in itself. He alone lives of and from Himself. All other beings live by virtue of the influx (or inflow) of life from Him. So the seed from the human father is only a *receptacle* of life. No human father gives life to his children. The only father who does that is the Lord our Heavenly Father. All that a human father does is provide and transmit a finite receptacle of life, and that finite form goes on receiving life in a finite way even when transmitted into the womb of the mother.

The seed from the father contains an offshoot from the father's soul. This offshoot is the soul of the potential offspring. The father's soul is finite, a receptacle of life; so too is the offshoot. The physical seed or semen is simply the carrier—the means of transmitting the soul. Having accomplished its use, the seed is cast off by the new soul, by the soul of the potential new being. This new soul is the means of directing the formation of the embryo. But it is *only* a means. Actually, it is *life from the Lord* that directs the formation and growth of the fetus in the womb. Life flowing in from the Lord, focused and channeled in an individual way by the new soul, is the force that directs the growth of the babe in the womb, the physical material being supplied from the body of the mother.

Life from the Lord is, of course, something above nature, something supranatural. This is why science, patiently and faithfully following its own proper methods and thereby limiting itself to nature and natural things, has never identified the force that directs growth, not only embryonic and fetal growth, but every other kind of growth. Nor will it ever be able to discover it while it is loyal to its own proper sphere: the natural and physical. There is more to life than merely the physical, but science is limited to the physical; the best of scientists admit this limitation. By the same token, religion has its limitations or limits, in the sense that its proper sphere is those parts of our life that are above the natural plane and cannot be discovered by scientific observation. Each discipline has its limits and its own foundation of truth.

Science is founded upon observation of the natural world; that is its criterion of judgment, its test of truth, its limit. Religion is founded upon what is revealed by the Lord about the things *above* the range of our physical senses, things that we would never know if the Lord did not reveal them. This is its proper criterion of judgment, its test of truth, and its limit.

Neither foundation of truth can *by itself* give us the whole truth concerning the Lord's universe: the natural world and the spiritual world. But both *together* give us the complete picture: religion supplies information about what is above nature, while science reveals the mysteries of the natural world by using its own method, sense observation. There need be no antagonism or contention between them, for they are two parts of one whole. This is true not only in general but also in particular, even with regard to the virgin birth.

Having seen that there is a supranatural element in every human conception and birth—that the Lord is indeed our Heavenly Father, the real agent every time a child is born, with the human parents merely cooperating or *pro*creating—we can now see what was similar and what was different in the virgin birth.

The only thing that distinguished the virgin birth from any other birth was the lack of seed from an earthly father, and consequently the lack of any finite *receptacle* of life, a human soul from an earthly father. There was no finite form *receiving* life from the one source of life. There was nothing like that acting as a means of fertilizing the ovum in the womb of Mary, as in the case of the subsequent children born of Mary, who were fathered by Joseph. The ovum was fertilized by the Divine Life itself!

So the angel Gabriel had said to Mary, "The Holy Spirit will come upon you, and the power of the Highest will overshadow you" (Luke 1:35). In fact, the angel went on to say, "Therefore, also, that Holy One who shall be born of you, shall be called the Son of God," meaning the offspring of the Divine Soul, thus the body of the Divine Being. Here was the Divine Being Himself, the Creator of the universe, forming a body for Himself in the womb of the virgin Mary, as He had foretold that He would do. "Behold, a virgin shall conceive and bear a Son, and shall call His name Immanuel" [that is, God with us] (Isaiah 7:14).

Because in the birth of the Lord there was no *human* father—for Mary "did not know a man" (Luke 1:34)—there was therefore a most significant difference between the heredity of the Lord on earth and that of an ordinary human being. In the *Arcana Coelestia* 1573:3–4, Swedenborg explains:

> No human being can possibly be born of another human being without thereby deriving [hereditary] evil. But the hereditary evil derived from the father is more internal, and remains to eternity, for it cannot possibly be eradicated; *but the Lord did not have such*

evil, because He was born of Jehovah the Father, and thus as to internal things was Divine or Jehovah. But the hereditary evil from the mother belongs to the external man; this did exist with the Lord . . . Thus was the Lord born as are other men, and had infirmities as other men have. That He derived hereditary evil from the mother is clearly evident from the fact that He underwent temptations; no one can possibly be tempted who has no evil; it is the evil in a person that tempts, and through which he is tempted. That the Lord was tempted, and that He underwent temptations a thousandfold more grievous than any man can ever endure; and that He endured them alone, and overcame evil, or the devil and all hell, by His own power, is also evident [from the Gospels].

The Lord had no tendencies or inclinations toward evil from any human father because the virgin Mary "did not know a man." But because she was a normal human being, she had and she transmitted *tendencies* toward evil, which the Lord in the flesh inherited. Of course, as it is explicitly taught further on in the passage just quoted, "the Lord had no evil that was actual, or His own, as He also says in John: 'Which one of you convicts Me of sin?' (8:46)" (*Arcana Coelestia* 1573:8).

The Lord did inherit *tendencies* toward evil, but no actual evil. Actual evil is evil in act, resulting from *yielding* to the inherited inclinations to be delighted by evil. He received these tendencies from His human mother, but only good from His Divine Soul, which was and is the Father.

In summary, the Creator Himself came on earth as the Redeemer, and this coming was achieved with the cooperation of the virgin Mary. The virgin birth was the same as any other birth, but in one respect it was also different: life came not through the receptacle of a human father, but directly from the very source of life itself.

The Lord came "to subjugate the hells." We cannot understand this without knowing the general principles of life in the *spiritual* world from which He came.

3

THE SPIRITUAL WORLD

In My Father's house are many mansions.

John 14:2

The concept of a spiritual world distinct from the world of nature is basic to all religion. In addition to belief in God, what makes a religion to be a religion, and what distinguishes it from a system of ethics or morality, is the idea of a spiritual world in which we are to live after the death of our body—a spiritual world where the Lord is and from which the Divine influence goes forth.

Both the Old and the New Testaments presuppose a spiritual world quite distinct from the natural world, although there is obviously some kind of communication between them, by means of human minds.

The first verse of Scripture declares: "In the beginning God created the heavens and the earth" (Genesis 1:1). In the original Hebrew, it does actually say "the heavens," not "the sky," for which there is another word altogether. A separate world is also clearly indicated in the following passages:

> Know therefore this day, and consider it in your heart, that the Lord Himself is God in heaven above, and upon the earth beneath: there is none else. (Deuteronomy 4:39)

> But there is a God in heaven who reveals secrets, and He has made known to the king Nebuchadnezzar what shall be in the latter days. (Daniel 2:28)

> The Lord is in His holy temple, the Lord's throne is *in heaven*: His eyes behold, His eyelids try the sons of men. (Psalm 11:4)

> Forever, O Lord, Your Word is settled in heaven. (Psalm 119:89)

There are also many cases in which a man or a number of men appeared and disappeared suddenly. This can hardly be explained without a belief in another world (see Genesis 18:3; 19:1; Exodus 3:2; Numbers 22:22 ff.). Angels also appeared to Joshua, Gideon, Manoah and his wife, Samuel, Elijah, Daniel, and Zechariah.

In the New Testament, an angel appears to Zacharias and to Mary, and a multitude of them appear to the shepherds (Luke 1:11, 26–38; 2:8–14). John on the Isle of Patmos was "in the spirit" (Revelation 1:10) and saw many things in that spiritual world. The whole Book of Revelation describes events in the spiritual world. In the case of the Transfiguration, Peter, James, and John saw Moses and Elijah (long since dead), who then disappeared when the disciples' spiritual eyes and ears were closed once more (Mark 9:1–8). All these cases indicate the presence of another world.

There are also several phenomena that are inexplicable apart from belief in another world: the burning bush (Exodus 2:3), the pillar of cloud (Exodus 13:21), the glory filling the tabernacle (Exodus 40:34), the writing on the wall at Belshazzar's feast (Daniel 5:5).

From sense observation and experience, we can all know about the natural world and its laws. Scientific investigation is discovering more and more about the way the natural, physical world and the physical body work. The natural world is the body's world.

It is where our bodies are. The laws of the natural world and the laws of the physical body are one and the same. We can discover these laws by using our eyes, ears, and other sense organs, and by forming conclusions on the basis of what we have sensated.

But, obviously, the *spiritual* world does not operate according to the same laws as the natural world. It is not the world of the body. It is the world of the *mind*. In fact, it is the world in which our minds are at this very moment. Although the mind is the means by which we are conscious of the natural world, the truth is that our mind is not spatially in the natural world at all. If it were, we could see, touch, and feel it by physical means. We all know by experience that we cannot do that, yet we are all equally well aware that each one of us has a mind. It is made of *spiritual* substance, not *physical* matter. It is not to be confused with the brain, which is part of the body and can therefore be sensed in the natural world by physical means.

But the mind is different. Being in the spiritual world, it operates according to spiritual laws. In order to understand the spiritual world, we need to understand the mind or spirit, and vice versa.

Whether we say "mind" or "spirit," we mean the same thing. The only possible difference is that we usually use the word *spirit* when referring to a mind that has been separated from the physical body at death. After death, the mind is usually called the spirit, hence the term *spiritual*, pertaining to the spirit. The difference between the natural world and the spiritual world is exactly the same as the difference between the body and the mind. It is important to remember this when thinking about the spiritual world. Everything happens there according to the laws of the spiritual world, according to the laws of the mind. This is exactly the kind of thing that happens in our own mind.

An example of the similarity between the laws of the mind and those of the spiritual world is the law that "thought brings presence." This is what happens in the mind. Our friends can be present in our thoughts; thinking of them makes them present in our minds.

"Thought brings presence" is also a law of the spiritual world. When we think of a person, he or she appears instantly if the Lord wills it, if some good may be brought out of it. In both the mind and the spiritual world, thought brings presence. The Lord's presence with us is possible only by thought and visualization. If the Lord is invisible to our mind, or vague and a mystery, we cannot think clearly of Him. He cannot be as present to us as He would be if we could think of Him clearly. The quality of the thought determines the quality of the presence.

The laws of the mind and of the spiritual world are quite different from the laws of the natural world. In our minds, we can defy time and space, traveling around the world in no time at all. We can think of places physically located on the other side of this world, but in mind or spirit, we can be there in literally no time.

There is actually no time or space in the mind, although there appears to be. We can think of things in our mind as being higher or lower, occurring before or after, being quick or slow. But this difference does not depend upon the movement of the earth around the sun as it does on the natural plane. It is all a matter of the state of our mind.

For example, if we are enjoying ourselves, time passes with incredible rapidity. But if we are waiting for someone to come to the telephone, for instance, a minute can seem like an hour. Time is a matter of state. Space in the spiritual world and in the mind is also a matter of state, as we can see from several literal statements in the Word of God, but especially from this parable in the Gospel of Luke:

> There was a certain rich man who was clothed in purple and fine linen and fared sumptuously every day. And there was a certain beggar named Lazarus, who was laid at his gate, full of sores, desiring to be fed with the crumbs which fell from the rich man's table; moreover the dogs came and licked his sores. And it came to pass that the beggar died, and was carried by the angels into

Abraham's bosom. The rich man also died and was buried. And in hell, he lifted up his eyes, being in torments and saw Abraham afar off, and Lazarus in his bosom. And he cried out and said, Father Abraham, have mercy on me, and send Lazarus, that he may dip the tip of his finger in water and cool my tongue; for I am tormented in this flame. But Abraham said, Son, remember that you in your lifetime received your good things, and likewise Lazarus evil things; but now he is comforted, and you are tormented. And besides all this, between us and you there is a great gulf fixed; so that those who want to pass from here to you cannot, nor can those who want to come from there pass to us. Then he said, I pray you therefore, Father, that you would send him to my father's house; for I have five brothers, that he may testify to them, lest they also come into this place of torment. Abraham said to him, They have Moses and the prophets; let them hear them. And he said, No, Father Abraham: but if one went to them from the dead, they will repent. And he said to him, If they do not hear Moses and the prophets, neither will they be persuaded, though one rose from the dead." (Luke 16:19–31)

Note that Abraham and the beggar appear to be higher than the rich man, who, being in hell, had to lift up his eyes to see them. There is also a great gulf fixed between heaven and hell to separate them. But obviously, all these things represent outwardly certain differences in the states of mind of the people mentioned.

That parable is unusual in this: it is the *only* one set in the *spiritual* world. All the other parables of the Lord have as their setting life in the *natural* world. He taught us many lessons about life in the spiritual world by comparing it with life in the natural world. But on this occasion, He chose to set His parable in the spiritual world itself. By doing this, He made it possible for us to learn a great deal more than is usually supposed about our life after death, simply by studying and reflecting on what is said in the literal statements in the Divine Word.

One of the outstanding characteristics of all the Lord's parables is that they are so true to life. From our experience of life in this world, we can readily understand the natural meaning of these parabolic stories. We can see how accurate they are. This, of course, does not surprise us; after all, one would expect the Lord God of heaven and earth, the Fountain of Wisdom itself, the Creator, to speak only what is true and accurate.

If this is true of his *earthly* stories, in which there is a heavenly meaning, why would it not be equally true of the one parable in which He describes explicitly something of our life in the spiritual world?

We raise this point because it has sometimes been doubted whether this account of the life after death is trustworthy, since it is "just a parable." We are well aware of the natural world and the laws by which it operates, but the spiritual world is on another plane of existence. For the vast majority of people today, it is beyond our experience. We have to rely on what the Lord has revealed about it by means of His servants, the prophets and disciples, who were Divinely raised up to set forth a knowledge and understanding of that world as He has revealed it to them. This parable is a case in point.

But can we think that the Lord would deceive us in His account of life in the spiritual world? Why would He give us false or misleading information about that life? Does He not want us to know about that life and believe in it? How inexplicable it would be if the Lord were to give us some information about it that was unreliable. Surely, we can trust God's Word.

There are many things that could be said about this parable from the Gospel of Luke. But what we want to notice at the moment is the obvious teaching that there are three regions of the spiritual world. Two of them are familiar to us: heaven (meant in the parable by "Abraham's bosom") and hell. But in between them is another region meant by "the great gulf": the world of spirits.

The spiritual world, with its three regions, needs to be put in its proper place in relation to the Lord and to the natural world. The diagram below compares the universe as a whole (a macrocosm) to a human being—a little universe or world (a microcosm).

The Microcosm and the Macrocosm

Humankind	The Universe
(Microcosm)	(Macrocosm)
SOUL	GOD
(receptacle of life)	(life itself)
MIND	SPIRITUAL WORLD
(organ of consciousness)	Heaven
	World of Spirits
	Hell
BODY	NATURAL (physical) WORLD

God is the *soul* of the universe, the source of life—in fact, life itself. The *spiritual world* (consisting of heaven, the world of spirits, and hell) is the *mind* of the universe.

The *natural world* is the *body* of the universe. In a human being, there is a perfect image of the macrocosm—the big world. A human being is a microcosm—a little world, an image of the universe as a whole. A human being has a soul, which, in relation to the mind and body, is like God in that it rules the mind and the body. By "the soul," we mean a receptacle of life, that spiritual organ in us that receives life directly from God. It is the part of us that is nearest to God, the first part of us to be touched by life flowing in from Him. It is nothing physical; it is a *spiritual* organ made of spiritual substance. Everyone—without exception, whether good or evil—has this spiritual organ, this receptacle of life called the soul.

But we are never aware of it or of what is happening there. It is always above our awareness. What would be the consequence if we were aware that life is flowing into our soul?

Obviously, we would not feel free. We would feel as if we were being pushed around, like a robot or machine. In order for us to feel free and be an image and likeness of God, we must never be aware of this life flowing into our soul. We can never sensate it. We can come to know about it only through Divine revelation. We cannot learn about it from below, looking up. That is contrary to the Divine order or way of operating.

There is another reason, too, for its being above our power to change. Our soul must ever remain unpervertible, always in a state of order. This is true even with an evil person who denies the very existence of such a soul and even denies the existence of God. Everyone must be free to go on receiving life, and for that reason, the Lord has provided a spiritual organ as a receptacle of life for everyone.

Beneath the soul is the mind—also a spiritual organ, but an organ of consciousness[1] or awareness. That is where we are; that is where we live. If you tell me what kind of a mind you have, you are telling me what kind of a person you are.

The mind, then, is the organ that makes us aware of the natural world while we have a physical body. But after the death of the body, we become aware of the spiritual world and cease to be aware of the world of nature. Death is nothing but a transfer of consciousness. In summary, then, the soul dwells above the spiritual world just as God dwells above it; the mind lives in the spiritual world, and the body in the natural world.

The three regions of the spiritual world (heaven, hell, and the world of spirits) need to be considered in order.

Heaven

Heaven is inhabited entirely by people who have lived on some earth in the universe. No angels were created in the beginning. The Book of Genesis, in describing the seven days of creation, does not mention the creation of angels, but only of human beings. If angels

---

[1] We are not speaking here of conscience, which is sometimes confused with consciousness. Consciousness means being aware, while conscience refers to choosing between right and wrong.

were created "in the beginning," why was this most important piece of information not clearly stated in the creation story in Genesis 1? Furthermore, human beings were created in the image and likeness of God (Genesis 1:26). Can we think, then, that angels are *more* than an image and likeness of God?

The book of Revelation makes it clear that the angels themselves reject the idea that they are superior to human beings and thus worthy of adoration:

> And I fell at his feet to worship him. And he said to me, See that you do not do that: I am your fellow servant, and of your brothers who have the testimony of Jesus. Worship God. (Revelation 19:10)

> And I, John, saw these things, and heard them. And when I had heard and seen, I fell down to worship before the feet of the angel who showed me these things. Then he said to me, See that you do not do that. For I am your fellow servant, and of your brothers the prophets, and of those who keep the sayings of this book. Worship God. (Revelation 22:8–9)

The Book of Revelation also speaks openly of "the measure of a man, that is, of the angel" (21:17). Further evidence is the Lord's testimony in the Gospel of Luke:

> Those who are counted worthy to attain that indefinite time, [eternity] and the resurrection from the dead . . . are equal to the angels; and are the sons of God, being the sons of the resurrection. (Luke 20:35–36)

From all this we can conclude that no one is born an angel; everyone has to be *reborn* an angel. Consequently, everyone who is now in heaven lived at one time as a man, woman, or child on some earth. They are now in heaven because while they lived on earth, they were *prepared* for heaven, cooperating with the Lord. They learned to love Him and to love the neighbor as themselves, which made them angelic—"equal to the angels," equal to those already living in heaven. They had obeyed the Two Great Commandments because that was the Lord's will. This is the purpose of life—to be reborn an angel.

Just being in heaven does not make heaven a kingdom of the Lord any more than merely having people in a church makes a church a kingdom of the Lord. What makes a church a church—and what makes heaven to be heaven—depends upon the kind of people who are there. The criterion is the extent to which they receive the love and the wisdom coming from the Lord. Receiving what comes from the Lord is what makes heaven; rejecting that is what makes hell.

From the Lord's saying, "The kingdom of God is within you" (Luke 17:21), we can safely conclude that heaven is essentially a state of mind. However, this state of mind is manifested as a place or a region for the simple reason that the whole spiritual world is a *representative* world. What we really feel and think in our minds is *re-presented*, projected outwardly there in visible form. For example, if a person has a beautiful mind, that beauty will be reflected in his or her surroundings. The Garden of Eden, which represents a heavenly state of mind, was so beautiful because it manifested outwardly that beautiful state of mind where people love the Lord first and foremost and their neighbor as themselves. On the other hand, if a person has an ugly, petty, or nasty mind, that will be reflected in ugly surroundings. Hell therefore looks hideous. Our predominant state of mind—whether good or evil—creates our environment in the spiritual world. "The kingdom of God is within you."

The qualities that make up that kingdom are described in several places in the Divine Word. Psalm 15 asks: "Lord, who shall abide in Your tabernacle? Who shall dwell in Your holy hill?" The question is, "Who is going to live in heaven?" The Psalmist gives this answer:

> He who walks uprightly, and works righteousness, and speaks the truth in his heart. He who does not backbite with his tongue, nor does evil to his neighbor, nor takes up a reproach against his neighbor; in whose eyes a vile person is despised; but he honors those who fear the Lord; he who swears to his own hurt and does

not change; he who does not put out his money to usury, nor take a bribe against the innocent. He who does these things shall never be moved. (Psalm 15:2–5)

Such people shall never be moved out of heaven because they are heavenly. They have all the heavenly qualities. Psalm 24: 3–5 is similar:

> Who shall ascend into the hill of the Lord? Or who shall stand in His holy place? He who has clean hands and a pure heart, who has not lifted up his soul to vanity, nor sworn deceitfully. He shall receive the blessing from the Lord, and righteousness from the God of his salvation.

The heavenly qualities that must be within us if we are to be part of the Lord's kingdom could therefore be listed in this way:

- *Walking uprightly*—doing what is right, fair, and just in all our dealings
- *Speaking the truth in our hearts*—being completely honest with ourselves and with others; speaking the whole truth
- *No backbiting with our tongues*—refusing to slander or defame
- *Doing no evil to our neighbor*—individually and collectively, for the neighbor is not just an individual but the whole community, the common good
- *Not taking up a reproach against our neighbor*—that is, refusing to treat a good person (a neighbor) disgracefully
- *Scorning the life of a vile person*—instead, honoring the life of those who have concern (or holy fear) for the Lord's welfare
- *Compelling ourselves to keep our promises to the Lord*—even when the promptings of our natural man cause this to hurt
- *Being constant* rather than fickle
- *Not looking for a reward*—a return on our investment when we do some good deed
- *Refusing to be swayed by personal considerations*—to avoid doing an injustice to the innocent
- *Having a pure heart*—acting from pure motives
- *Shunning vanity and conceit*
- *Shunning all kinds of deceit*—especially false oaths

In the New Testament—in the Sermon on the Mount (Matthew 5:2–12)—the Lord, while setting forth the blessings of heaven, added the following list of blessed qualities that make heaven or the kingdom of God:

- *Poverty of spirit*—a realization of how little we know and understand of the Lord's wisdom
- *A spiritual kind of mourning* brought on by facing realistically our lack of goodness
- *The mildness of charity or goodwill* toward the neighbor
- *A hunger and thirst after righteousness*—a spiritual appetite for finding the Lord's Divine order and living according to it
- *Mercifulness*
- *Purity of heart*
- *Peaceableness*—the quality of being a peacemaker
- *A willingness to be persecuted* by those who hate the Lord's way of life
- *A willingness to follow the Lord* even when ridiculed by others

This is by no means an exhaustive list of the qualities of mind that make up the kingdom of God. The list is endless, for the Divine Word from beginning to end speaks of nothing else, often by contrasting opposite qualities. But the qualities just enumerated do give us some idea of what the Lord meant when He said, "The kingdom of God is within you" (Luke 17:21).

However, it is equally true that the kingdom of hell may also be in us. Hell, like heaven, is essentially a state of mind, although the very opposite of a heavenly one.

Hell

Hell is inhabited by men and women who have rejected the Lord and His commandments. They have chosen *deliberately* not to live according to those commandments. They *knew* what they should do, but they habitually said to themselves: "It's too much trouble. I prefer to please myself. It's much more fun that way." Rather than *give to* the world (which people who are predominantly charitable want to do), they love themselves first and foremost and want to *get from* the world, especially status and position for the *sake* of status and position or wealth for the *sake* of wealth. They have rejected the Lord deliberately, by free choice. By their habits of life in this world they have come to love themselves and the world supremely (see Jeremiah 13:23).

We all have some love of self and some love of the world. Otherwise we would be hermits! But the people who are in hell are those who love self and the world above all else. They think of themselves first. That is what they love supremely.

This kind of love, when it predominates, is what makes hell to be hell. Hell is essentially an attitude of mind or a predominant state of mind that is seen as a place, as heaven is. However, as the manifestation of a very hideous, ugly kind of mind, hell is seen as a very ugly place, at least to the angels, who see everything in the light of heaven. But those who are in hell, being quite immersed in the hellish state of mind, do not see the ugliness. They feel quite at home in hell because their outward environment corresponds to their inner ugliness.

If the people in hell were brought into heaven, they could not stand it. They could not even breathe in the atmosphere. The breathing there would be different; the pulse rate would be different. The atmosphere of heaven would be oppressive to them because hellish people are immersed in loves entirely opposite to those enjoyed by heavenly people. Because they love what is the very opposite of heavenly bliss, they would gasp for breath in heaven, like fish out of water. They simply could not stand the company. As the Book of Revelation says, "And [the evil] said to the mountains and rocks, 'Fall on us, and hide us from the face of Him who sits on the throne, and from the wrath of the Lamb'" (Revelation 6:16).

Is there anything comparable to that phenomenon in this world? Surely we have all felt uncomfortable—ill at ease—in a certain gathering because of the atmosphere. We have felt out of our element. We have not felt at home, not because we felt we were better than the other people there, but because the atmosphere felt foreign. It was not what we like. It may even have been the opposite of what we like. We felt *different* from the prevailing atmosphere.

It would be a similar case to that of hardened criminals who, having deliberately chosen a life of crime, are forced to sit down and listen to a lecture on religion, on heaven, or on charity toward the neighbor. How would they feel? They simply could not sit still. They would writhe and squirm because what they love is so contrary to the prevailing atmosphere surrounding them.

Our parable about the rich man and Lazarus teaches the same thing. The two men were poles apart. Being clashing opposites, they could never dwell together. There was an unbridgeable gap or gulf between them, between heaven and hell.

All the evils forbidden in the Ten Commandments and elsewhere in the Divine Word are what make hell to be hell. They are the opposites of the good qualities that make heaven:

- *Living dishonestly,* working injustices
- *Deceiving one's self* and striving to deceive others
- *Using the God-given gift of speech* to abuse verbally, even to slander and defame
- *Harming the neighbor*—not only the neighbor individually but also the common good; doing harm to society in general (to say that such evils are antisocial is to put it mildly; they are against society because they are all for self)
- *Treating good people disgracefully,* but honoring and exalting evildoers
- *Never compelling one's self against evil*—in fact, never allowing oneself to suffer at all, being entirely unwilling to suffer[2]
- *Being changeable,* acting according to one's whims and fancies

---

[2] A person suffering in hospital is called a patient—from a Latin word meaning "to suffer." Impatient people are unwilling to suffer—especially to suffer a delay in getting what they want. That is another characteristic of hell—being predominantly impatient, that is, unwilling to suffer.

- *Always expecting some benefit or advantage to self,* and being unwilling to help unless that is guaranteed
- *Succumbing to bribes and other corruption* to the detriment of the innocent
- *Having an impure heart* and a mind consumed by vanity or self-conceit
- *Swearing deceitfully,* laughing at perjury
- *Lacking any poverty of spirit,* being rich in one's own conceits
- *Lacking all spiritual mourning,* being convinced of one's own righteousness
- *Lacking the mildness of charity* and being filled instead with the harshness and cruelty of evil
- Having no appetite for the kind of life that comes from obedience to the Lord's commandments
- *Being cruel and merciless*
- *Having nothing but ulterior motives*
- *Being a disturber of the peace* rather than a peacemaker
- *Reveling in persecuting and ridiculing* those who strive to live by the Lord's principles—rather than being persecuted for righteousness' sake

This partial list gives an insight into what hell is like. It allows us to see what hellfire really is. It is not a fire that is outside of us, a physical fire that burns our bodies; rather, it is the fiery, raging passions of evil that burn within our minds. The kingdom of hell can be within us. When we think of the hot and burning emotions that can rage inside us, we can understand why it is said in Isaiah: "Wickedness burns as a fire" (Isaiah 9:18).

Wickedness does indeed burn like a fire. Surely all the evils condemned by the Lord in the Ten Commandments are hot and burning and insatiable. What other kind of hellfire can there be? What other kind of hellfire need there be? What else is it but our burning, all-consuming selfishness that results when we have completely and deliberately rejected the Lord—our fiery passions and ambitions, our burning lusts, our heated arguments, our hot anger and fiery tempers, our smoldering resentment as we burn for revenge? These are the fires of self-love burning within us—the fires of hell.

If these fiery loves of hell are what characterize us in this life, then we will still have them inside us after death to eternity unless we repent and change our ways here, which, of course, we are quite free to do. If hell continues to rule inside us here, we will also have it outside of us—all around us—hereafter. If heaven reigns inside us here, it will be all around us hereafter. We will continue to be just the same kind of person after the death of the body.

After all, what is death? What part of us can die? Only the body, and our body is not the person. It is like a topcoat, a garment that is very useful for life in this physical world. We could not do without it. We must have some physical organism that will be effective on this physical plane. That is why we have a physical body.

But when it has outlived its usefulness, when, in the Lord's good judgment, it is time to separate our mind or spirit from the body, it is cast off. It is no longer of use, nor do we ever resume it again. There is no need for that (see 2 Samuel 12:23; 14:14; Job 7:8–10; Hebrews 9:27). Death is simply like shedding our topcoat.

Are we any different when we take off our topcoat? No, not a whit. So after death, we are no different from what we are now in our minds. The mind or spirit is the person. What habitually takes place in our minds determines what kind of character we have, and are, and will be. Nothing is changed by the death of the body. We will remain to eternity the same as we have chosen to become. "In the place where the tree falls, there shall it lie" (Ecclesiastes 11:3).

Understanding this, we can see that, in effect, we judge ourselves. We find our eternal lot among those whose predominant, ruling, characteristic loves are the same as ours, whether good or evil. Although the judgment after death is sometimes depicted in the Bible as a kind of tribunal with God as judge, this is written according to the appearance. In reality, we judge ourselves. We are making our choices every moment of our waking hours in this life.

We are free to choose on which side of the gulf we wish to remain to eternity (see Deuteronomy 30:15–19).

The punishment of hell, then, is self-inflicted. The Lord casts no one into hell, but many people find their eternal abode there, of their own free choice. Punishment in hell is self-inflicted because it is the nature of selfishness or evil to bring punishment down upon its own head. What makes hell a place of torment and of no peace is that everyone there wants to rule over everyone else, having his or her own way. The selfish love of dominating is what makes hell to be hell. Heaven may be the dominion of love, but hell is the love of dominion (*Spiritual Experiences* 5000).

If you want to know what hell is, just imagine a society where everyone, without exception, burns with the ambition to rule and dominate by any means whatsoever. Once people have climbed to the top, they are filled with mortal dread because they know that everyone else lusts after their position and are probably plotting to topple them. They also know that they have made many enemies, whom they climbed over and trampled upon on the way up. They can trust absolutely no one.

Imagine a society where you could not trust *anyone*, where you knew that everyone was out to get your position. No wonder, then, that the Divine Word says that "there is no peace for the wicked" (Isaiah 48:22; 57:22). There can be no peace (unity) because evil people are out solely for themselves. That is hell—the real hell—here and hereafter.

The resemblance to the lives of gangsters is not surprising, since that is nothing other than hell on earth—the supreme and classical receptacle of hell.

It would surely be the height of cruelty to make people on opposite sides of that great gulf live together to eternity. What more refined kind of torture could there be than to make angelic people endure those devilish people, and to make those devilish people endure the angelic people? The pain would be about equal on both sides. It would simply be intolerable. So it is really an act of Divine mercy that hell is provided by the Lord for those who do not want to be in heaven. It is the inevitable consequence of the very real freedom of choice that the Lord has given us all.

The Lord never interferes with that freedom of choice. If we choose hell, the Lord respects that choice, but He never abandons us. To eternity, He strives to save us from a lower hell, from worse and worse evils. As the Psalmist says: "Where shall I go from Your Spirit? Or where shall I flee from Your presence? If I ascend into heaven, You are there: if I make my bed in hell, behold, You are there" (Psalm 139:7–8).

Some people object to this on the ground that those in hell would be happy among themselves. True, it is the greatest happiness that they can have. But compared with heavenly happiness (which goes on developing and growing to eternity), the so-called happiness of hell is misery itself. It has to be continually restrained. It cannot be allowed to go beyond certain limits. It is not free to grow to eternity. Understanding the qualities of hell, the selfishness and burning hatred embodied there, can we imagine people in that state being happy together? "There is no peace for the wicked" (Isaiah 48:22).

The whole purpose of life is to choose, freely and rationally, on which side of the gulf we wish to be forever. But that choice is made here and now in every decision we make. It cannot be left until we come into the spiritual world; it is too late then. It is too late to change what we have come to love as a matter of habit. That, after all, has determined our basic character (Jeremiah 13:23).

Having seen in a general way the nature of the real heaven and the real hell, we need to consider the intermediate region that is neither heaven nor hell—the world of spirits.

The World of Spirits

The conclusion that there is an intermediate state—neither heaven nor hell but a state in between them—has been based so far on the

Lord's parable in Luke 16. The Book of Revelation teaches the same thing. In the first chapter the Apostle John, on the Isle of Patmos, says he was "in the spirit." He was aware of the *spiritual* world but not of the *natural* world because his spiritual eyes and ears were opened. This state of mind was very common with the prophets of old.

In Revelation 4, he beholds a door opened in heaven and is invited to go up into heaven. The fact that he had to go up surely indicates that he was beneath heaven; but there is nothing to suggest that he was in hell. There must, therefore, be an intermediate region between heaven nor hell. In that intermediate region he also saw the Holy City, New Jerusalem, coming down from God out of heaven (Revelation 21:2).

This intermediate region—the great gulf between heaven and hell—is called "a valley" by the prophet Joel in the Old Testament; he saw "multitudes, multitudes, in the valley of decision!" (Joel 3:14). This "valley of decision" is a place or state of mind in which we choose where we belong—in heaven or in hell.

There is a need for such an intermediate region. Very few people today are fit for either heaven or hell immediately after death. Some people are indeed completely angelic at death; they are the same within as they are outwardly, angelic inside and outside, fit for heaven immediately after death. They have long since been living according to the Two Great Commandments—love to the Lord and charity toward the neighbor—because these commandments are the Law and the Prophets, the Word of the Lord. But such people are comparatively few.

Similarly, there are some people who are so completely evil, so blatantly evil, and such dedicated evildoers that they freely go immediately to hell after death. They make no attempt to cover up what they love; they have no shame; they have no self-imposed restraint. They openly do what is evil whenever possible, and advocate doing evil. They *love* evil. They are ready for hell immediately after death.

However, as far as the majority of adults is concerned, we are for the most part a disconcerting mixture of good and evil qualities. We may be predominantly good, loving the Lord more than self and loving the neighbor more than the world. We may be quite charitable, generally speaking. But we may also still have some of the qualities of hell, which are incongruous. They do not belong to our heavenly character. There is a discrepancy that has to be removed so that our whole mind reflects our good character.

On the other hand, some people *appear* to live an impeccable life, but underneath, in their motives and secret thoughts, they are devilish. They mask their underlying evil and selfishness with a very pleasing exterior, with courtesy and the appearance of kindness, giving the appearance of loving the neighbor. Again, the outside does not match the inside. There is a discrepancy between them.

The law of the spiritual world is that there can be no such discrepancy between people's inner thoughts and feelings and their outer words and deeds. In the Gospel of Luke, the Lord says that "there is nothing covered that shall not be revealed, nor hidden that shall not be known. Therefore whatever you have spoken in darkness will be heard in the light, and what you have spoken in the ear in closets shall be proclaimed upon the housetops" (Luke 12:2–3).

Some provision must be made—some place, some state of mind—for this revelation of the real person to take place, where the superficial blemishes of a good person may be removed and the good-looking outward characteristics of a hypocrite may be sloughed off. This process is really a preparation either for heaven or for hell, taking place after death in "the valley of decision," "the great gulf fixed" between heaven and hell. This intermediate region, the world of spirits, is where spirits—all people who have recently died—immediately congregate.

At first, in this place, we seem just the same outwardly as we were in this world. We look the same, we sound the same, we act in the same way, we *are* the same. We all gather together according to our natural, worldly interests, as we did in this world, good and evil together. In this world, the characters of people with a common interest in football, for example, could be quite varied or even opposite. At a football game, a good person could be seated next to a criminal and not know it. It is like this when we first wake up in the world of spirits: we are outwardly the same as we are in this world.

But gradually we come into that second stage just described, where our real character is revealed, and people begin to separate. Evil people can no longer stand the company of those who are predominantly good, and they freely go off to the place provided for them, where they may be with similar people and be themselves. The Lord never casts anyone into hell. Nor is anyone cast into hell against his or her own wishes. People freely choose to go there for eternity because, while living on earth, they have chosen hell in preference to heaven in most situations. The Lord provides us all with opportunities to choose heaven or hell. That is why He said through Moses, "See, I have set before you this day life and good, death and evil. . . . I call heaven and earth to record this day against you, that I have set before you life and death, blessing and cursing" (Deuteronomy 30:15, 19).

But the Lord wants us to choose heaven rather than hell, so He concludes, "Therefore choose life, that both you and your descendants may live" (30:19).

If we have chosen life (eternal life or heaven) most of the time, then that is what we will choose in the world of spirits, "the valley of decision." Similarly, if we have chosen death and evil at every opportunity, we judge ourselves to hell.

It is worth noting that both the rich man and Lazarus found their final abode very soon after the death of their bodies. There is no reference at all to their being obliged to wait until the day of judgment before their final destiny was decided. We can conclude, then, that we are judged individually, soon after our arrival in the other world. We do not have to wait somewhere or other until a general judgment for all takes place. This, of course, should not surprise us. After all, did not the Lord Himself say to the penitent thief on the cross, "This day you shall be with Me in paradise" (Luke 23:43)? *This day.* Once again, there is no indication of waiting for the last day—doomsday—before a decision is made. How, then, did the idea ever come into existence and be accepted that we would have to wait until a general judgment takes place, and that our physical bodies would have to be resurrected?

That idea seems to have arisen from a misunderstanding of the Scriptures—from a failure to take into account *all* of the passages on the subject, and also from the practice of applying everything to *this* world and not to the spiritual world. The spiritual world, surely, is the only world in which a judgment—individual or universal on all who have ever lived—could possibly take place. When we consider the multitudes of people involved, to say nothing of the limitations of space that characterize this natural world, we can see that a universal judgment in this world is quite an impossibility, contrary to the Divine laws of order.

This was well understood by the Apostle Paul in his First Letter to the Corinthians. He insists that there is "a natural body, and there is a spiritual body," and that "a natural body is sown, a spiritual body is raised" (15:44). Also, "flesh and blood cannot inherit the kingdom of God, nor does corruption inherit incorruption" (15:50). Consequently, "we shall not all sleep, but we shall all be changed. . . . For this corruptible must put on incorruption, and this mortal must put on immortality" (15:51–53). Why would this change be necessary if the judgment took place in this natural world? Paul clearly sees that we need to be changed by putting off our *physical* bodies in order to be judged in the *spiritual* world.

The spiritual world does not operate according to the natural world's laws of time and space, but according to the same laws as the mind, or spirit. Therefore, there is no limitation to the number of people who can be summoned together in the spiritual world, which is why the spiritual world—the mind's world—is the scene of the judgment after death. Surely, the mind is to be judged and not the body, which has never of itself done anything good or bad. It is merely an obedience to the mind. The mind is the person.

Failure to understand this has led to the idea that the general judgment after death takes place in the *natural* world. Human nature is very apt to lead us to falsely believe that the *body* is the person, not the mind or spirit. Each one of us is a mind or spirit clothed with a body. The body is simply added to allow us to be useful in this world.

Thinking that the body is the person also leads to the conclusion that when the body dies, the person is either extinct forever, or that if people are ever to live again, they will have to take on their old, worn-out body once more. Thus the doctrine of a resurrection of the physical body came into existence and kept alive the idea of another life at a time when people found it hard to believe that the mind is the person. This happened despite the fact that the Bible never speaks of the resurrection of dead bodies, or corpses. It speaks of the resurrection of the dead, but never of cadavers.

Our minds are even now in the world of spirits. The spiritual world is not far away somewhere; it is all around us. It is as near to us as our minds are near. We can even feel its presence, its atmosphere. The powerful atmosphere we experience sometimes when watching a play comes from nowhere else but the spiritual world. The sense of peace or the feeling of being uplifted experienced in a particularly moving service of worship comes from the spiritual world—from heaven.

While we are on earth, encompassed in our physical bodies, our minds are midway between heaven and hell—in the world of spirits. We can look up to heaven or down to hell. That is how our freedom of choice is maintained. The Lord keeps us in equilibrium, in balance, so that it is just as possible for us to look up as to look down.

If that balance were ever endangered, then the Lord would have to intervene on a grand scale in order to restore it. Otherwise, we would have no freedom of choice; we would all be hell-bound.

To understand why the Lord intervened two thousand years ago at precisely that time—not a hundred years earlier or a hundred years later—we need to understand the state of the spiritual world as a whole (and that of the world of spirits in particular) at that time.

4

THE SPIRITUAL WORLD TWO THOUSAND YEARS AGO

Multitudes, multitudes in the valley of decision.

Joel 3:14

The Lord always provides a church on earth to ensure that there is a link between heaven and earth, so that the Lord's will may be done on earth as it is done in heaven. When that happens, heaven and earth are working together in conjunction.

If it ever happened that there was not one person left reading the Word of God, believing it, and trying to live according to it, then that link would be broken. Hell would take over, with nothing to counteract it. No force for good would exist that could possibly curb the flood of evil and falsity that would result if the church were ever destroyed, if the Lord's kingdom disappeared entirely from the earth.

The Lord does not allow that to happen, by providing that somewhere there will always be a remnant of a church, the remains of a church that can maintain a link between heaven and earth by teaching the Word of the Lord. Two thousand years ago, the Jewish Church had the most current form of the Word—the Old Testament.

Yet at that time, the Pharisees—the leaders of the Jewish Church—were neither teaching the Word of God nor living according to it. In the Gospel of Mark, chapter 7, the Lord told them that they preferred their own traditions to the Word of God. They had found fault with the Lord because His disciples did not wash their hands before meals, although the Word says nothing about doing so. The Pharisees had invented that regulation. So they asked the Lord, "Why do Your disciples not walk according to the tradition of the Elders, but eat bread with unwashed hands?" (Mark 7:5). In response, the Lord berated them for putting the tradition of the Elders above the Word. "All too well you reject the Commandment of God, that you may keep your own tradition . . . making the Word of God of no effect through your tradition" (Mark 7:9, 13).

He then gave an example that amply justified His rebuke, reminding them of the commandment "Honor your father and your mother" (Exodus 20:12). In the beginning, the people applied that commandment to life by providing for their parents in old age when they could no longer fend for themselves. This application of the commandment to honor father and mother was clearly a very practical and humane one. It had a good effect.

However, in course of time the Pharisees and the leaders of other sects of the Jewish Church began to put their own self-interest first, declaring that it was perfectly appropriate for people to donate to the temple the money set aside for their parents. They could say, "It is Corban" (a gift), and be absolved from the obligation of providing for their parents—at least, in the amount of the gift. This may have been good for the temple and those associated with it, but it was disastrous for the parents. It destroyed both the spirit and the letter of that commandment, for, as the Lord went on to point out to the Pharisees and the Scribes: "You no longer let [a person] do anything for his father or his mother" (Exodus 20:12).

That is just one example of the general tendency among the Pharisees to prefer their own man-made rules to the Word of God. They were virtually burying the Word under their traditions.

If the Word of God is the link between heaven and earth, it is only by living according to the order described in the Word that there can be any conjunction with heaven. If, however, the Word is not being taught—if human traditions are being taught instead— then that link becomes very tenuous indeed. The Lord came on earth to restore that link. He came to restore a belief in the Word and a life according to it.

Among the faithful remnant of good people who were the sole means of preserving that link were Joseph and Mary; Mary's cousin, Elizabeth, the wife of Zechariah and the mother of John the Baptist; the disciples of John; and those who were willing to be baptized by John and follow his teaching, which sought to bring people back to the Word of God. Also among them was the aged Simeon:

> This man was just and devout, waiting for the consolation of Israel, and the Holy Spirit was upon him. And it was revealed to him by the Holy Spirit that he would not see death before he had seen the Lord's Christ [the Lord's Anointed]. So he came by the spirit into the temple: and when the parents brought in the Child Jesus, to do for Him according to the custom of the law, then he took Him up in his arms, and blessed God and said, "Lord, now You are letting Your servant depart in peace, according to Your Word: for my eyes have seen Your salvation, which You have prepared before the face of all peoples; a Light to bring revelation to the Gentiles, and the glory of Your people Israel." (Luke 2:25–32)

Also to be numbered among the remnant of the church would be Anna, a prophetess, who also came to the temple at the same time as Simeon and likewise gave thanks for the coming of the Lord, "and spoke of Him to all those who looked for redemption in Jerusalem" (Luke 2:36–38).

But hypocrisy was rampant among the church leaders of that time, as is manifest in many places in the Gospels, especially in Matthew 23, where the Lord openly revealed the leaders' true characters. For example, the Lord said of them to the disciples: "They bind heavy burdens and hard to be borne, and lay them on men's shoulders: but they themselves will not move them with one of their fingers" (Matthew 23:4). He denounced them to their faces, saying: "Woe to you, Scribes and Pharisees, hypocrites! For you make clean the outside of the cup and platter, but inside they are full of extortion and self-indulgence. . . . Even so you also outwardly appear righteous to men, but inside you are full of hypocrisy and lawlessness" (23:25, 28). As He said, "All their works they do to be seen by men" (23:5). So He denounced them seven times in this chapter as "hypocrites" (see 23:13–15, 23, 25, 27, 29). In addition, He characterized them as "blind guides" (23:16), "fools and blind" (23:17, 19), "serpents, brood of vipers" (23:33), and "whitewashed tombs which indeed appear beautiful outwardly, but inside are full of dead men's bones, and all uncleanness" (23:27). Elsewhere, He cited as evidence their practice of sounding a trumpet on the street corners when they did any good deed so that they would have glory from men (Matthew 6:2), and praying on the street corners to be seen by men and considered devout (6:5), and making a great show of fasting so that everyone might know of it (6:16). But surely the most damning condemnation of all was this: "You shut up the kingdom of heaven against men; for you neither go in yourselves, nor do you allow those who are entering to go in" (Matthew 23:13).

The leaders of the Church were destroying the Church, preventing the good and innocent from entering into the Lord's kingdom. As a result, the Lord had to intervene and mount a rescue operation to salvage those who were savable. For it is quite beyond doubt that the Pharisees wanted to rule and *continue* to rule; they wanted to keep forever the rigid grip they had upon the people. The Gospels report that the people did not dare oppose them, for fear of being disgraced and cast out of the synagogues (John 9:22).

When the multitude rejoiced to see the Lord enter Jerusalem in the manner of a king and waved palm branches to welcome Him, the Pharisees were stricken with panic and begged the Lord to silence His disciples (Luke 19:39). But when this attempt at suppression failed, they said among themselves: "You see that you are accomplishing nothing. Look, the world has gone after Him" (John 12:19). Their hateful, unreasoning, unreflecting jealousy and their love of worldly status are likewise revealed in their pathetic lament: "What shall we do? For this Man works many signs. If we let Him alone like this, everyone will believe in Him: and the Romans will come and take away both our place and nation" (John 11:47–48).

"Our *place* and nation." Was ever a group more tellingly convicted out of its own mouth? Their status and their own were what they loved and feared to lose.

A complete study of the Gospel references to the Pharisees reveals that their qualities could be listed in this way:

- A merely natural understanding of spiritual things
- A rigid and burdensome interpretation of the Divine law, especially with regard to observance of the Sabbath
- A stultifying worship of human traditions
- Covetousness and avarice
- A love of honor and glory in the eyes of the world
- Empty, eye-catching piety and fasting
- Self-righteousness and self-congratulation, accompanied by a cruel contempt of others in comparison with themselves
- A constant belittling of what is good
- A denial of the Lord's Divinity
- Chronic fault-finding, with a desire to discredit
- Chronic complaining and discontent

- An outward appearance of righteousness masking an inner hypocrisy and filthiness
- A refusal to enter more deeply into the good affections and true thoughts of the Lord's kingdom, thus retarding the spiritual progress of others whom they taught
- A frightening love of dominating over others for the sake of self and the world

These were the qualities of the teachers in the Jewish Church, "blind leaders of the blind" (Matthew 15:14). Is it any wonder that hypocrisy abounded?

Would such hypocrites pass through the first stage of the world of spirits at the normal pace, or would it take a long time for their real character to be revealed? Obviously, it would take much longer for hypocrites to realize their true qualities, because they have for so long practiced the nefarious art of covering up their real selves. They have no desire to reveal their inner thoughts and intentions. Hypocrites are deceivers; therefore, they will remain for an exceedingly long time in the first stage of the world of spirits, appearing outwardly the same as in the world.

But what would be the effect of a *great number* of hypocrites coming into the world of spirits after death? It would paralyze the whole process of judgment. The world of spirits would be, so to speak, clogged up. As one member of an Inquirers' Class put it, "It would be gridlock!" So the prophet Joel, prophesying "the day of Jehovah," the coming of the Lord in Person to judge the Jewish Church, sees "multitudes, multitudes in the valley of decision! For the day of Jehovah is near in the valley of decision" (Joel 3:14). There were *multitudes* there because the process of judgment, which normally takes place on an *individual* basis, was severely slowed down. Too many hypocrites remained in the first stage, retaining their ability to appear outwardly righteous and thus deceive people.

Consequently, most of them, being leaders of the Church, tended to gather around themselves a coterie of *good* people, simple people who could be deceived because they did not have as much learning as these leaders. These congregations of good people, ruled over by hypocritical instructors and leaders, are called "false heavens." The good people, listening to the advice and discourses of these "blind leaders of the blind," thought they were in heaven because these masters seemed to be so well instructed and so wise. But the reality was very different. These were "false heavens," destined to be dispersed at the general judgment that would occur when the Lord came. The *real* heaven would never be destroyed. Why would the Lord destroy what He had labored so hard to create?

Yet the Scriptures do speak about a new heaven and a new earth replacing the former ones, which "shall not be remembered, nor come upon the heart" (Isaiah 65:1; 66:22) and about "heaven and earth" fleeing away from the face of Him who sat upon the "great white throne" (Revelation 20:11). In the Book of Revelation, the Apostle John reports seeing "a new heaven and a new earth: for the first heaven and the first earth had passed away; also there was no more sea" (Revelation 21:1).

Attempts to understand these passages literally, as if they referred to physical things, are beset with a thousand difficulties. For instance, how would the physical earth flee away or pass away, and to what purpose would this be done? Why would the Lord want to destroy the real heaven? Why would the world's oceans need to disappear?

This is prophecy, and the language of prophecy is precisely the same as the language of parable. We all know that in a parable, a physical object represents some spiritual reality.

The "earth" does not mean the mineral kingdom, but the Lord's kingdom on earth. Similarly, "heaven," where the angels live, is the Lord's kingdom in the spiritual world. So in the Lord's Prayer, we pray, "Thy will be done, as in heaven, so in earth" (Luke 11:2, King James version).

But when we read of heaven or earth passing away or being rolled away, the Lord's kingdom is not meant. The subject is those "false heavens" already mentioned, those congregations in the world of spirits where hypocrites pose as angelic, "heavenly" masters and mesmerize the trusting good people who are the members of their "church" or "the earth." In this way, the hypocrites kept simple, good people in a state of personal adulation, taking away worship from the Lord, which the hells love to do. These gatherings are what had to be swept away at the general judgment.

The procedure is this: the good are first rescued from the clutches of those who are interiorly evil and, after suitable preparation and instruction, are taken into heaven. "They are equal to the angels" (Luke 20:36). The evil have their real character exposed and go where they belong, among their own people. This is also what is meant when Satan is said to have fallen from heaven (Luke 10:18). How could what is hellish ever have come into the real heaven, and how could what is heavenly ever fall out of heaven? This is declared impossible in the parable of the rich man and Lazarus (Luke 16:19–31). The false heavens of hypocrites are what pass away.

These hypocrites were all hell-bound and subconsciously in league with the societies of hell (or simply "the hells"), being like their ambassadors, controlled by the hells. The loves from which they subconsciously acted were the same as those that drive the hells—love of self and love of the world. These were their ruling or predominant loves, universally present in everything they felt, thought, did, and said, no matter how righteous their outward appearance may have been.

Since these pharisaic leaders were really tools of the hells, it is easy to see how the inhabitants of hell were having a tremendous influence in the world of spirits. That is why it is said that "the hells had increased to such a height as to fill the whole world of spirits" (*True Christian Religion* 121). They were having a far greater influence there than they should have had.

Bearing in mind that the world of spirits is where our minds are, what would be the effect of this state of affairs upon the human race?

The first effect was that it almost cut off spiritual enlightenment completely. It was as if a huge cloud had been placed between heaven and people on earth. This dark cloud in effect blotted out the spiritual light and warmth that should go forth from heaven to warm and enlighten human minds. But with the world of spirits so full of unjudged people—both the hypocrites and the enthralled good people—only a very little spiritual light (by which we see the truth or reality) was able to filter through. It was being dissipated and diffused in its passage through the world of spirits. The light of heaven was only just filtering through, just enough to keep the human race somewhat human. Even that light was in danger of fading out.

That is why, two thousand years ago, there was such gross darkness with regard to spiritual things. The ideas about religion that prevailed were in the lowest degree natural and sensual. Take the Greek gods, for example. There were multitudes of them. The Romans likewise were pagans. The only place where there was any knowledge at all of the real God was in the Jewish Church, but the Old Testament had been twisted and perverted; it was being used to serve merely natural and worldly ends. Consequently, there was gross darkness everywhere with regard to spiritual things, and even with regard to the moral virtues. Morality in the broad sense of the word was quite feeble at that period in history, though some few rays of light were shining among thinkers who were able to rise above the prevailing darkness.

Gross injustices occurred even on the civil plane. History records quite graphically the cruelty and oppression of those times, the feeling of hopelessness that reigned, the injustices done to the few faithful, honest people. Especially in the Roman empire, the "might is right" philosophy prevailed.

But the Lord always has to preserve a balance between the influence of heaven and that of hell, so that our free choice may operate. The extent to which the balance is tilted in favor of hell is the extent to which our freedom is in jeopardy. If it were ever to reach the point where hell dominated, we would have no freedom of choice at all. The tendency to be taken over by the inhabitants of hell would become irresistible. Choosing heaven—that is, the heavenly way of life—would become impossible.

This was on the verge of happening. The evidence for this is quite dramatic: the instances recorded in the New Testament of demon possession. The inhabitants of hell could actually take possession of a person on earth. Anyone able to take complete possession of our mind can, at the same time, take over our body, because the body is really only in obedience to the mind (*Apocalypse Explained* 10:712). What the mind does, the body follows.

Since the influence of the inhabitants of hell had invaded the world of spirits, the hells were having an undue impact upon the minds of people on earth, as our minds are in the world of spirits. In some instances recorded in the New Testament, the inhabitants of hell had completely taken possession of the minds and bodies of people on earth—against their will. In Luke 8, we find a representative case:

Then they sailed to the country of the Gadarenes, which is opposite Galilee. And when [Jesus] stepped out on the land, there met Him a certain man from the city who had demons for a long time. And he wore no clothes, nor did he live in a house, but in the tombs. When he saw Jesus, he cried out, fell down before Him, and with a loud voice said, "What have I to do with You, Jesus, Son of the Most High God? I beg You, do not torment me!" For He had commanded the unclean spirit to come out of the man. For it had often seized him, and he was kept under guard, bound with chains and shackles; and he broke the bonds, and was driven by the demon into the wilderness. And Jesus asked him, saying, "What is your name?" And he said, "Legion," because many demons had entered him. And they begged Him that He would not command them to go out into the abyss. Now a herd of many swine was feeding there on the mountain. And they begged Him that He would permit them to enter them. And He permitted them. Then the demons went out of the man and entered the swine, and the herd ran violently down the steep place into the lake and drowned. When those who fed them saw what had happened, they fled and told it in the city and in the country. Then they went out to see what had happened, and came to Jesus, and found the man from whom the demons had departed, sitting at the feet of Jesus, clothed and in his right mind. And they were afraid. (Luke 8:26–35)

No wonder they were afraid! Imagine this awe-inspiring event, perhaps the most dramatic case on earth of a person being entirely taken over. This man had no control; he was utterly obsessed, yet he was brought back to his right mind. In fact, the account goes on to say that he wished to follow the Lord, but the Lord said, "Return to your own house, and tell what great things God has done for you" (8:39).

Was this man possessed against his will? Was he perhaps an evil man who *summoned* the presence of the devils?

That does not seem to be the case. When restored to his right mind, this man wanted to follow the Lord. It seems much more likely that he was possessed against his will and incited by the devils to his self-destructive acts.

If he *was* possessed against his will, if even good people could be controlled involuntarily, the consequences would be enormous. If this condition became general, if most or all people were possessed by the inhabitants of hell, the human race would inevitably have been destroyed physically. Even innocent children were beginning to be possessed. Something had to be done at once.

In the second representative case—in Mark 9—an innocent child is possessed against his will:

Then one of the multitude answered and said, "Teacher, I brought You my son, who has a mute spirit. And wherever he seizes him, he throws him down: he foams at the mouth, gnashes his teeth, and becomes rigid. So I spoke to Your disciples, that they should cast him out, but they could not. . . . Then they brought him to Him. And when He saw Him, immediately the spirit convulsed him, and he fell on the ground and wallowed, foaming at the mouth. So He asked his father, "How long has this been happening to him?" And he said, "From childhood. And often he has thrown him both into the fire and into the water to destroy him. But if You can do anything, have compassion on us and help us." (Mark 9:17–18, 20–22)

This is a classic case of involuntary possession. Some have wondered whether perhaps this might rather be a case of epilepsy. The symptoms are similar except for one thing: An epilepsy patient does not attempt to throw himself or herself into fire or into water. This destructive element is missing from that ailment. In the biblical incident, however, it was predominant. This marks it as a clear case of possession—involuntary possession.

When even innocent children were being possessed against their wills and were led to self-destruction, something had to be done on a large scale. The Lord simply had to intervene in order to preserve human freedom of choice and make it possible for those who wanted to choose heaven to be in a position to do so, and to save the human race from both spiritual and physical destruction.

It is understandable, then, that the Lord intervened in human affairs—came in the flesh—at this particular point in history.

The traditional explanation for the purpose of His coming on earth is that He came to take the punishment due to the human race by reason of the sin of Adam and Eve. According to this account, God the Father would have had to punish every human being because of the guilt inherited from Adam and Eve, as well as for their own actual sins, unless someone else took the punishment in place of the human race. To this end, so it is said, God the Father sent His Son (considered to be another separate Divine Person) into the world to be a sacrifice and atonement for the human race. But why this was not done centuries before is never explained. In fact, in this explanation of the Lord's advent and His work of redemption, there seems to be very little attempt, if any, to relate His intervention to the state of the world at the time.

The Lord delayed His coming until evil had reached its fullness or greatest height. When this could be tolerated no longer because of the danger to the people of both heaven and earth, the Lord had to intervene on a large scale.

5

REDEMPTION REVISITED

Redemption was a work purely Divine.

Emanuel Swedenborg
True Christian Religion 114

The Lord's taking on a human form and appearing in the flesh is called His *incarnation*, which simply means "taking on, or being manifested in, a body of flesh," according to *Webster's Dictionary.* The root meaning of the word comes from the Latin *caro, carnis*—flesh.

The Lord came to redeem. In ordinary usage, the word *redeem* means "to recover possession of by paying a specified sum" (*American Heritage Dictionary*). Applied to theological matters, it refers to the whole process by which the Lord bought back the human race from the brink of destruction when He came into the world—by paying a price.

Why Did the Lord Put on a Human Form?

The Lord intervened by taking on a human form, by being born into this world through the virgin Mary, one of the few faithful people remaining in the Jewish Church. But why was it necessary for the Lord to intervene in *this* way? Why could He not have restored the hells to their proper place in some other way?

In truth, there was no other way. If the Lord had become fully present in the world of spirits *as He is in Himself* and sought to drive back the hells, He would simply have destroyed them. It would have been as if the sun of this world, with its intense heat and light, had come close to this earth. Everything would have been burned up and annihilated. It would have been a similar case if the Lord had approached the hells as He is in Himself. He would have destroyed them.

Why, then, didn't He destroy the hells? Surely, that would have been one solution to the problem.

But let us consider. The Lord will never, under any circumstances, take away human freedom of choice, but honors and respects it absolutely and eternally. It is a very *real* choice that the Lord gives us. If we choose to reject Him, He allows us to do so. So it would have been against His Divine essence and character, against His own Divine order and way of operating, to destroy people because they had made the wrong choice when He had first given them the freedom to make that choice. Besides this, the Lord gives the gift of life to everyone born into the world. Anything that He gives stays given. He does not give with one hand and take away with the other. He does not give life to any individual in such a way that He would snatch it away if that individual did not follow the order of life for human beings. That is why even the devils of hell continue to receive the gift of life. The Lord never withdraws it. Consequently, it would have been against Divine order to destroy the hells.

The *only* solution was to veil over His Divinity by taking on a human nature. In this way, God could be present without destroying. His Divine presence could be, so to speak, tempered by the human nature surrounding His Divinity.

Another advantage of this solution was that His human nature could actually summon the presence of the inhabitants of hell, without destroying them. Because of the inclinations toward evil that He would inherit by taking on a human nature, He could, in fact, invite the presence of the hells. His *Divine* part could never be tempted, but His human part certainly could.

It is well known in the Christian world—even from the days of the early Christian Church—that the Lord was "tempted in all points as we are, yet without sin" (Hebrews 4:15). For the Lord's human nature to be tempted, He had to have the same subconscious communication with the various societies of hell that we all have. These societies of hell inspire evil desires and false thoughts. For this to be possible with the Lord, He needed to have in His human nature the usual tendencies or inclinations toward evil that everyone born into the world inherits. These tendencies toward evil were what attracted and summoned the presence of the hells. All this was achieved by the Lord's taking on a human nature by birth through the virgin Mary.

In the following passage from Swedenborg's *Arcana Coelestia* 1573:3–4 (Heavenly Secrets), the Lord's heredity is distinguished from that of an ordinary human being:

> No human being can possibly be born of another human being without thereby deriving evil. But the hereditary evil derived from the father is one thing, and that from the mother is another. The hereditary evil from the father is more internal, and remains to eternity, for it cannot possibly be eradicated; but the Lord did not have such evil because He was born of Jehovah the Father, and thus as to internal things was Divine or Jehovah. But the hereditary evil from the mother belongs to the external man; this did exist with the Lord. . . . Thus was the Lord born as are other men, and had infirmities as other men have. That He derived

hereditary evil from the mother is clearly evident from the fact that He underwent temptations; no one can possibly be tempted who has no evil; it is the evil in a person that tempts, and through which he is tempted. That the Lord was tempted, and that He underwent temptations a thousandfold more grievous than any man can ever endure; and that He endured them alone, and overcame evil, or all hell, by His own power, is also evident [from the Gospels].

To say that in His human nature the Lord inherited tendencies toward evil is not to say that the virgin Mary was an evil woman. Far from it; she was one of the remnant of the good in Israel. But everyone for generations back inherits *tendencies* toward evil, although not evils themselves. Tendencies toward evils are inclinations to delight in what is forbidden in the Divine commandments. No one is exempt from such tendencies, not even the virgin Mary. No one is ever the offspring of "an immaculate conception." Without inheriting from His mother such tendencies to evil, the Lord could never have been tempted. The hells could never have approached Him.

However, at no time did the Lord ever *yield* to the inclinations to evil that He inherited. He was tempted by means of them, but He never sinned. He was "without sin." He was therefore able to rebuke His accusers, saying: "Which of you convicts Me of sin?" (John 8:46).

The Two Results of the Lord's Victories in Temptation

What were the results of this incarnation, this coming in the flesh, this presence of the Lord God Himself, the Creator of the universe, in physical form?

The first result was that He was able, by means of victories in His often daily temptation struggles, to bring the hells under His yoke and control; He "came into the world to subjugate the hells"

(*True Christian Religion* 2). To subjugate is to "put under the yoke" and so gain control. From His own Divine power within, He was able to resist the devils or evil spirits, all of whom had once been evil people on earth. He was able to fight against them and reject their suggestions and strong urgings. If we wish to form some idea of the intensity of the Lord's temptation battles, we have to imagine the whole of hell, the whole assembly of evil people, with their hatred, malevolence, and cunning, continually urging and inciting. We can perhaps gain a very inadequate picture of what it must have been like by imagining the turbulent violence of a prison riot. But the Lord was able to combat the urgings of the hells, and also reject the false ideas that they continually presented to Him.

The greatest of all His temptations was a feeling of hopelessness, a feeling that the task was too great, that it would be impossible to save the human race. The intensity of any temptation can be gauged by the quality and intensity of the love that is attacked, all temptation being an attack upon our love. For example, we make a New Year's resolution to give up some bad habit. We now have a new love: the love of being rid of that habit. But the moment we make that resolution, it is attacked by spirits from hell who want to keep us in that old habit and weaken and destroy our new love. We feel that as a temptation, saying in our mind, "Do I really *want* to give it up? Is it really *possible* to do so?"

In the case of the Lord, it was His great love of saving the human race from misery and destruction, His *Divine and Infinite love*, that was incessantly attacked. This was the cause of His most excruciating temptation.

As the Lord fought against the societies of hell in turn and as He triumphed over them, He gradually restored them to their proper place. He repelled them and put them down. He restored order in the world of spirits, so that the warmth and light of heaven could once more flow down and be received by human minds. The whole spiritual world was, in this way, restored to a state of order. Human freedom of choice was rescued from destruction. All this is known as the Lord's work of *redemption*. To redeem is to regain possession, and the Lord did indeed regain possession of the human race. He rescued it from annihilation, and the price He paid for this was daily giving up merely human delights, and finally giving up life on the physical plane.

So that was one result of the Lord's victories in His temptations; He "subjugated the hells" and thus redeemed or saved the human race from physical, moral, and spiritual destruction.

The Second Result

The second result of His victories has to do with a change in the human nature that the Lord had taken on. When He repelled a society of the hells, He put that society back in its place. But at the same time, this made a profound change in His human nature. What had attracted a particular society of hell was a particular tendency toward evil that He had inherited in His human nature. When He repelled a society of hell, He also expelled the inherited tendency toward evil that had brought on the temptation. (This expulsion is represented in the second chapter of the Gospel of John, by the Lord's expelling the money changers from the temple, "the temple of His body," as it is called in John 2:21. They did not belong there and had to be driven out, just as hereditary evils had to be removed from the Lord's human part inherited from Mary.)

As He gradually expelled the tendencies to evil in His human nature, something from His Divine soul within flowed in to take their place. As each tendency to evil was expelled, some Divine goodness, something of His Divine love, flowed into His human part and took its place. Eventually, everything inherited from the mother Mary had been driven out so that Divinity could occupy even what before had been merely human and natural. *He was no longer the son of Mary.*

This is what is involved in the puzzling incidents recorded in the Gospels in which the Lord rejected Mary. For instance, it is said that when Jesus on the cross "saw His mother, and the disciple whom He loved [John] standing by, He said to His mother, 'Woman, behold your son!' Then He said to the disciple, 'Behold your mother!' And from that hour that disciple took her to his own home" (John 19:26–27).

Jesus was no longer the son of Mary, but fully the Son of God—the Divine offspring of the Divine Soul (the Father). He was the *Divine* human, His human level having become completely Divine. "The Lord from eternity, who is Jehovah, came into the world to subjugate the hells and to glorify His Human" *(True Christian Religion* 2). There are several references in the Gospels to this process of glorification, this process by which the Lord made His human level to be as Divine as His soul, especially in the Gospel of John.

One of the clearest instances is in John 12, where the Lord on earth said: "Now My soul is troubled; and what shall I say? 'Father, save Me from this hour'? But for this purpose I came to this hour" (12:27). This is a state of temptation. The Lord says He is troubled or disturbed. He cannot ask for this temptation to pass. He cannot ask His Divine part, which He calls "the Father," to spare Him this temptation because it was for the sake of achieving victories in temptation battles that He came into the world.

The Lord continues: "Father, glorify Your name" (12:28).

The "Name of the Father" when present on the physical plane was, of course, Jesus. Jesus is asking His Divine part to make His human level Divine, that is, to *glorify* it. See also John 17:1–5, where this is quite explicit. Our passage in chapter 12 concludes: "Then a voice came from heaven, saying, 'I have both glorified it and will glorify it again'" (12:28). Here we see that the process of glorification (making Divine) was gradual, just as the process of rebirth or regeneration (making spiritual) in us is gradual.

We may still wonder why the Lord had to die; why did He have to give up even His human body? The answer is that He had to give up everything from the mother Mary, including the flesh and bones. Even on the level of His human part, He had to become Divine and not be forever a *receptacle* of life. He had to become life itself. This the Lord had referred to earlier when He said, "For as the Father has life in Himself, so He has granted the Son to have life in Himself" (John 5:26). He was Divine from first to last, from the inmost to the outmost, from the highest to the lowest.

Yet why did He have to glorify His human level, making it Divine? The purpose of this was to ensure that the hells could no longer rise up out of their place. This is explained in the following passage, *Arcana Coelestia* 1820:5, where the subject is victory in our temptations:

> Victories are attended with the result that the malignant genii and spirits afterwards dare not do anything; for their life consists in their being able to destroy, and when they perceive that a man is of such a character that he can resist, then at the first onset they flee away, as they are accustomed to do when they draw near to the first entrance to heaven, for they are at once seized with horror and terror, and hurl themselves backward.

If this is the case with merely human temptations, how much more true is it of the Lord's victories in His temptations? In the presence of the *Divine* resistance, the hells could do nothing but flee away to their proper places. They were to be *forever* held in subjection. They could never again rise up and threaten human freedom of choice unless the human race, using that freedom Divinely restored and maintained, *chose* to invite them to do so. They could no longer do what they had been doing prior to the Lord's intervention: taking possession of people on earth against their will.

The two results of the Lord's victories in His battles against the hells were these: First of all, He reduced them to order—which was His work of redemption—and at the same time and by the same means He guaranteed that they would remain in their place by making His human level Divine also. By glorifying His human level—so that He was Divine from first to last, so that even on earth

He had all power—the Lord was able to be present with the human race in a new way, in a fuller, more intimate way than He previously could. He could be present even on the physical plane and in His own Human form. This was another purpose of His coming in the flesh: He could be fully and actually present. This was not possible before His coming in the flesh. Before that pivotal event, the only way to communicate with the human race was comparatively remote and indirect. He had to make use of an angel, whom He would fill with His spirit to such an extent that the angel spoke entirely from the Lord, his own personality having been put to sleep. This happened at various times with several different angels. In each case, the angel was called in both the Old and New Testaments "the Angel of the Lord," and sometimes "Jehovah." For examples, see Genesis 22, Judges 6, and Matthew 1.

This account of the Lord's reason for coming, and of His work of redeeming or saving humankind, is quite different from what has usually been taught. The Lord did not save us by His *death*. He saved us by His *life*, every moment of it. While He lived on earth the Lord was continually battling against the hells (Luke 4:13). By His life the Lord accomplished the redemption of the human race, but by His death He completed the process of glorifying His human part (or making it Divine) so that His work of redemption might be permanent. His death was the last of His lifelong temptations.

Saved from What?

The Lord did not save us from the consequences of sin—from the punishment due to sin. This, after all, is impossible. Punishment is inherent in sin. It is self-inflicted. If we break the laws of the spiritual realm, the consequences are just as inevitable as when we break the laws of the physical realm—unless we repent, that is, unless we change our way of life. Let us recall that the laws of the spiritual world really are *laws;* they are not mere rules and regulations, which can sometimes be broken with impunity. They are laws, descriptions of how things happen on the spiritual plane, just as the laws of nature are descriptions of the way things happen on the physical plane. The Lord Himself reminded us of this when He said, "Whoever commits sin is a slave of sin" (John 8:34). The reference, of course, is to committing sin *habitually*. It is what we are *accustomed* to do that determines whether we are good or evil (Jeremiah 13:23).

If we break any law, natural or spiritual, the consequences are inevitable. Therefore, the Lord could not (because He would not) buy back the human race from the consequences of sin. What He did was buy us back or rescue us from inevitable bondage to the hells, from being robotlike slaves of those in hell because of involuntary demon possession. He did not save us from the consequences of sin; He saved us from being compelled to sin. He restored human freedom of choice, which was in jeopardy. In doing this, He saved the human race from physical, moral, and spiritual destruction.

Relevance Today

Obviously, the Lord's work of redemption two thousand years ago does have relevance for us today, because without it "no mortal could have been saved." We simply would not be here today if the Lord had not redeemed the whole human race.

But it is possible to see another aspect of this relevance. It arises from the fact that the process by which the Lord made His human part to be Divine is the prototype of the process by which we human beings, as would-be disciples of the Lord, are regenerated—that is, how from being merely natural in our desires and thoughts we gradually become spiritual in quality. This regeneration or rebirth of the natural mind is a process, not an event. In fact, it is an image and likeness of the Lord's glorification. And the means are the same: victories in temptation battles. But it is the Lord who wins the battles for us. He fights for us in our temptation combats. Knowing this, we see the continuing relevance of the Lord's work of redemption.

This is brought out in a most illuminating and moving passage in Swedenborg's *True Christian Religion* 599. It describes how the Lord, who once worked a general redemption for the whole of humankind, continues to redeem each one of us individually even today. This passage shows, perhaps more than anything else, how relevant, practical, and important our ideas of God and of redemption are. It reads as follows:

> In the conflicts or temptations of men the Lord works a particular redemption, as He wrought a total redemption when in the world. By conflicts and temptations in the world the Lord glorified His Human, that is, made it Divine; in like manner now with man individually, when he is in temptations, the Lord fights for him, conquers the evil spirits who are infesting him, and after temptation glorifies him, that is, makes him spiritual. After His universal redemption the Lord reduced to order all things in heaven and hell; with man after temptation He acts in a similar manner, that is, He reduces to order all the things of heaven and the world that are in him. After redemption the Lord established a new church; in like manner He also establishes what pertains to the church in man, and makes him to be a church in particular. After redemption the Lord bestowed peace upon those who believed in Him, for He said: "Peace I leave with you, My peace I give to you: not as the world gives I give to you" (John 14:27). Likewise He gives to man after temptation a sense of peace, that is, gladness of mind and consolation. From all this it is clear that the Lord is the Redeemer forever.

Those Who Believe in Him

We should now have a clearer idea of the first statement in the faith of the New Church in its universal form: "The Lord from eternity, who is Jehovah, came into the world in order to subjugate the hells and glorify His Human; without this no mortal could have been saved." There remains now the last sentence of the statement, which reads, "and those are saved who believe in Him" (*True Christian Religion* 2).

Actually, we will be looking into that last sentence in some detail in Chapter 8 in the statement that "saving faith is to believe in Him." But it is important to point out at this stage at least something of what is involved in believing in the Lord.

It is not simply a matter of *saying* that we believe in Him. It is not just a matter of the intellect, of the lips and the lungs. Nor does "saving faith" come all at once, on one glorious day. It comes progressively, "little by little" (Deuteronomy 7:22).

"Saving faith" is the kind of faith that saves a person from a hellish kind of life. It is the faith that belongs to charity and also comes from it—the kind of faith that a charitable person has. The way charitable people believe—the kind of insight that they have—is markedly different from the merely theoretical kind of faith of uncharitable people. We have as much of faith as we have of charity. The two go together. A little charity means a little faith, a wavering faith. Much charity means much faith. This is because, as we read in *Arcana Coelestia* 3893:12, "Faith is the eye of love." In other words, faith is love or charity *seeing*.

Summary of Part One

In this opening section of the new view of Christianity, we have discussed the importance of the idea of God and of redemption, and how a mistaken idea of these two subjects can destroy the effectiveness of the church so that it can no longer carry out its appointed task of being the link between heaven and earth. We have also seen in a general way that Jesus is Jehovah in His own human form, which He took on by means of birth through the virgin Mary, so that the subject of the virgin birth was involved in our statement.

We discussed some of the general teachings about the spiritual world, seeing that one of the urgent reasons for the Lord's coming on earth was the state of the spiritual world two thousand years ago, when the influence of the hells penetrated into the world of spirits, thus having an insidious effect upon the human race on earth at that time. We saw how the Lord could save the human race only by taking on a human nature that could veil over His Divinity and yet attract the hells so that they could be fought and conquered.

We saw two effects of the Lord's victories in His temptation-battles: first, that He conquered the hells and brought them to heel, ending involuntary demon possession; and second, that He glorified (or made Divine) His human part, in this way keeping the hells under control to eternity.

We saw that in doing this, the Lord saved the human race from physical, moral, and spiritual destruction. This is why he is called the Savior and Redeemer.

We also saw that just as the Lord carried out a *general* redemption of the human race two thousand years ago, in the same way He carries out a *particular* redemption or salvation for any individual person who is willing to cooperate with Him. His way of working in a particular redemption is the same as in the general redemption.

Finally, there was a brief mention of what real belief is, and that it must come from the heart, from obedience to the Lord's commandments.

In Part I, we have been considering the *Lord's* part in our redemption and salvation. In Part II, we will be looking at some particulars about what we human beings need to do in order to cooperate with the Lord in His work.

PART
TWO

INTRODUCTION

In Part II, we will look more closely at the particulars of the new view of Christianity. *True Christian Religion* 3:2 enumerates them as follows:

1. God is one, in whom is a Divine trinity, and the Lord God Savior Jesus Christ is that one.

2. Saving faith is to believe in Him.

3. Evils should not be done because they belong to the devil and are from the devil.

4. Good things should be done because they belong to God and are from God.

5. These things should be done by man *as if* from himself; but it should be believed that they are from the Lord with man and by means of man.

The first two belong to faith, the next two to charity, and the fifth to the conjunction of charity and faith, thus of the conjunction of the Lord and man.

Our discussion is becoming increasingly practical. We need to begin, however, with matters of faith, the things that are to be believed because they are true. These form the framework for considering matters of charity, the things that should be done because they are good. *How* these things are to be done is the focus of the final chapter.

6

HOW TO UNDERSTAND
THE TRINITY

*God is one, in whom is a Divine trinity, and the Lord God
the Savior Jesus Christ is that one.*

Emanuel Swedenborg
True Christian Religion 3:2

In order to see just what the Old and New Testaments actually say
on the subject of the God we are to worship, we will follow two
basic, common-sense rules:

1. We will gather *all* the passages on a subject, or at the very least
   a *representative* sampling of them.

2. As the basis and starting point, we will use only explicit statements that can have only one meaning.

The passages on the subject easily divide themselves into
two groups that at first sight seem to conflict. The first seems to
teach that God the Father (or Jehovah of the Old Testament) is one

person, and Jesus, the Son of God, is another person, quite distinct and separate. But, as we saw in Chapter 2, there is also a second group of passages that teach that they are one and the same, that Jehovah of the Old Testament and Jesus of the New are indeed the same Person. Obviously, these two groups of teachings have to be considered and reconciled if we are to discover the Divine Word's complete teaching.

Here are some examples of passages in the first group:

Jesus said: "I proceeded forth and came from God; nor have I come of Myself, but He sent Me." (John 8:42)

The Son can do nothing of Himself, but what He sees the Father do. (John 5:19)

You are the Christ, the Son of the living God. (Matthew 16:16)

This is My beloved Son in whom I am well pleased. (Matthew 3:17)

My Father is greater than I. (John 14:28)

No one comes to the Father except through Me. (John 14:6)

Make disciples of all the nations, baptizing them in the name of the Father, and of the Son, and of the Holy Spirit. (Matthew 28:19)

In this last passage, not only does it seem that the Father and the Son are distinct, but also that there is yet a *third* Divine Person or Being, the Holy Spirit.

If we were to consult only passages like these and ignore all the others that seem to conflict with them, we might come to the conclusion that there are three persons in God. This is extremely puzzling to people of a reflective turn of mind, because their common sense tells them that there simply *cannot* be three Divine Persons or Beings, because that is the same as saying that there can be three infinites, or three gods.

This puzzle plagued me as a fifteen-year-old, at the age when many young people reflect on what they have been taught and seek to understand it. The Lord Himself taught us to pray to "Our Father in heaven." But the question that bothered me was this: "When I am praying to the Father, am I leaving Jesus—and the Holy Spirit—out in the cold?" The task of uniting three distinct Divinities into one God is the ultimate in frustration.

But the way out of this frustration is to notice that it is never explicitly stated in so many words that the Father and the Son are *two* distinct persons. That is never said. But it was taken for granted by the councils of the early Christian Church from A.D. 325 onward, and has been unthinkingly accepted as the orthodox Christian faith itself. But search as you will, you will *never* find a passage that says explicitly that the Father and the Son are two, or that anyone who has seen the Son has yet to see the Father. As a matter of fact, you will find the very opposite, as we shall see in a moment.

Moreover, the second thing to be noted is that while it has usually been taken for granted that in these passages the terms *Father* and *Son* always refer to people, this is not necessarily the case. Do we not say in common speech, "The wish is *father* to the thought"? In the Word of God, we find a similar usage: "When he speaks a lie, he speaks from his own resources, for he is a liar and the *father* of it" (John 8:44).

From these considerations, we may see how risky it is to seize upon only one of the possible meanings of a term and build doctrine upon it. Even though common usage in ordinary conversation indicates that *father* and *son* refer to different people, if we assume that as a principle here, we will encounter severe difficulties when trying to understand the second group of passages, which teach that God the Father and God the Son are the same and the only Divine Person.

In the Old Testament, the Son is called "Mighty God" and "Everlasting Father" (Isaiah 9:6). Many passages say that there is only *one* Mighty God (Isaiah 43:10–11; 44:6; 45:21–22) and that He would Himself come into the world as the Savior (Psalm 9:18; Isaiah 25:9; 40:3, 5, 10). In the Old Testament, the Lord Jehovah says that He is the First and the Last. Yet in the New Testament, in the Book of Revelation 1:11, *Jesus* says He is the First and the Last. Since it is impossible to have two people being the first or the last, it must be the same Person who is described in both cases. The same conclusion was reached from the fact that Jehovah says He is the *only* Savior, yet in the New Testament, Jesus is frequently called the Savior. So the irresistible conclusion is that Jesus is Jehovah in human form.

In full agreement with this, in the New Testament we find the Lord Jesus Christ saying to the multitude, "I and My Father are one" (John 10:30)—not two, but one. Jesus did not say anything about being one in purpose, or any other such thing. He said simply *one*. In any case, His audience made no mistake about His meaning—the only possible meaning. They took up stones to stone Him, and when they were asked why, they replied, "Because You, being a man, make Yourself God" (John 10:33).

It is interesting that the Jewish Church, which rejected Him, understood what He was saying, but the Christian Church, which accepted Him, has not fully known Him.

Furthermore, in the first chapter of John, it is written:

> In the beginning was the Word, and the Word was with God, and the Word was God. . . . Everything was made by Him, and not one thing that was made was made without Him. . . . He was in the world and He made the world, and the world did not know Him. . . . And the Word became flesh and lived among us. (John 1:1, 3, 10, 14, *The Good News Bible*).

Here it is plainly stated that it was the Creator of the world who came on earth in the form of a man. That is why the Lord, when on earth, could say without blasphemy, "Before Abraham was, I AM" (John 8:58).

"I AM" can have but one meaning. It is Jehovah's name (Exodus 3:14). *Jehovah* means "being," the only Divine Being or life

itself. On this occasion also, the Jews understood the Lord to be saying, "I am Jehovah," and therefore they wished to stone Him for
blasphemy.

From all these passages, the teaching is manifest: Jehovah
(or the Father) and Jesus (the Son of God) are actually the same Divine Person. But it is in the fourteenth chapter of the Gospel of
John, above all, that this teaching is given its clearest expression.
Here, Jesus, having mentioned going to His Father, is misunder-
stood by both Thomas and Philip, who think that He is referring to
some other person. So Philip says, "Lord, show us the Father, and it
is sufficient for us" (John 14:8). In answering, the Lord removed the
misunderstanding: "Have *I* been with you so long," He asked, "and
yet you have not known Me, Philip? He who has seen Me has seen
the Father; so how can you say, 'Show us the Father'?" (14:9). Could
anything be more plain? What other Father can there be but the one
whom Philip's eyes were beholding?

Then the Lord went on to give an explanation that fur-
nishes the clue to understanding the whole doctrine. He said, "The
words that I speak to you I do not speak on My own authority; but
the Father who dwells in Me does the works" (14:10).

How are we to understand that? What is it in a human
being that dwells within, causes words to be spoken, and also does
the works? What else answers this description but the soul? It dwells
within, it causes words to be spoken, it does the works. What else
fits the description, in this case, but the Divine Soul? Is not the Divine Soul like a father to the body? Is not the body a kind of offspring from the soul?

When we see that *the Father* means "the Divine in itself" or
"the Divine Soul," and that *the Son of God* means "the Divine Body
visible to humankind" (together with the mind that grew up with
it), then at last we are in a position to understand something about
the Holy Spirit. In every person there is a trinity—a *human* trinity.
It is not a trinity of persons; humans do not consist of three persons
each. The human trinity is a trinity of parts: a trinity of soul, body,

and that intangible influence that flows forth from the union of soul and body. This spirit or influence going forth is approximately what is called, in popular language, a person's aura or personality. It is the atmosphere that emanates from the combination of soul and body, and that is what has an effect on other people. We have this trinity of soul, body, and influencing spirit because we are made in the image of God, and in God there is a Divine trinity: the Divine Soul, called the Father; the Divine Body, called the Son; and the Divine Influence or Spirit, called the *Holy* Spirit.

This understanding of the relationship between God and the Son of God is a real understanding because it throws light on the whole Word, both the Old Testament and the New. The real teaching of the Word becomes transparently clear when *all* the passages are considered and when those teaching unequivocally that there is but one God are taken as the basis, all others being interpreted in that light.

Now we can see where the obscurity, confusion, and mystery came from. It came from taking the *wrong* set of passages as the basis, that is, the first group we looked at, those that *seemed* to teach that there are two or three separate Divine Beings. In the new view of this subject, these passages can be understood in quite a different way:

"I came from God" (John 8:42)—the Body came forth from the Soul.

"The Son can do nothing of Himself, but what He sees the Father do" (John 5:19)—the Body can do nothing of Itself, but what it is directed to do by the Soul.

"You are the Christ, the Son of the living God" (Matthew 16:16)—the Messiah, the Body of the Divine Itself, which is life in itself.

"This is My beloved Son, in whom I am well pleased" (Matthew 3:17)—the Divine Body, in which it pleased the Lord to dwell while on earth.

"My Father is greater than I" (John 14:28)—the Soul is greater than the Body, since it formed and directed It.

"No one comes to the Father except through Me" (John 14:6)—just as we cannot know a person's soul except insofar as his or her body reveals it, so also the only way we can have any idea of the Divine Soul is by means of the Divine Body, which was visible to humankind. Or, as it is said in another place, "No one has seen God at any time. The only begotten Son, who is in the bosom of the Father, He has declared Him" (John 1:18).

In this view of the trinity, we are no longer obliged to picture more Divine Persons than one, nor more infinites than one. We see that it *can* be rationally understood. We can see that the Divine trinity is in the Lord Jesus Christ, just as the human trinity of soul, body, and spirit (or proceeding influence) is present in the body of every person. This idea seems to have been glimpsed somewhat among the early Christians, who, though commanded by the Lord to baptize in the name of the Father, Son, and Holy Spirit (Matthew 28:19), actually used a different formula: they baptized "in the name of Jesus Christ" (Acts 2:38; 8:16; 10:48), and so does the Church based on the new view of Christianity.

Note that the disciples were commanded to baptize "in the *name* (singular) of the Father, Son, and Holy Spirit," not in their *names* (plural) as would be the case with three separate beings. The disciples knew that the name of the Father, Son, and Holy Spirit was *Jesus.*

The idea of the Lord that the Apostles had is now restored and filled with details. In its general form, it is not new; it was there all the time, and it was summed up beautifully by Paul in one of his letters: "In Him [Jesus Christ] dwells all the fullness of the Godhead bodily" (Colossians 2:9),[1] that is, in bodily form.

This is the vision of the Lord that is possible again today. It is a concept that is capable of unceasing development, not one that

---

[1] The "Godhead" means Deity or Divinity (*Young's Analytical Concordance of the Bible*).

is stunted and stultified by the dogma of "a Divine Mystery." It allows everyone to picture the Creator taking on a frail human nature in order to be present more closely with humankind, a human nature that could be tempted and that could at last be glorified or made Divine, as Divine as His Soul, by means of victories in those temptation battles. That is why, at the end, Jesus could say to the disciples without blasphemy, "All authority has been given to Me in heaven and on earth" (Matthew 28:18).

SOME OBJECTIONS ANSWERED[1]

Those who are in doubt before they affirm are those who incline to a life of good.

Emanuel Swedenborg
Arcana Coelestia 2568:6

A common objection to the view of the Trinity set forth in the previous chapter is that it is nothing else than "Sabellianism," which is the understanding of the trinity advanced by Sabellius, a third-century theologian. Sabellius could see the impossibility of three separate Divine Persons or Beings. This would undoubtedly mean three gods, as God is a Divine Person and a Divine Person is God. So Sabellius propounded the idea that the Father, the Son, and the Holy Spirit were but three manifestations of the one God.

---

[1]For several of the ideas in this chapter, I have to thank the Reverend Samuel Noble in his "Appeal on Behalf of Swedenborg," 393ff.

That belief is more of an advance toward monotheism, but it still leaves unanswered the question, Who is this God of whom the Father, Son, and Holy Spirit are three manifestations? What is His name?

Only a moment of thought is needed to see how different the teaching of the new view of Christianity is, so there really should be no confusion whatever between the two beliefs.

The new view of Christianity teaches that the trinity is *in* the Lord Jesus Christ, who is the one and only God. "The Lord Jesus Christ" is the name of the God we worship in the new view of Christianity. He is not merely one part of a trinity of Divine Persons. The trinity is *in Him*, the Father being His Divine Soul, the Son the Divine Body, and the Holy Spirit the Divine Influence going forth. In other words, everything is centered in the Lord Jesus Christ; He is the visible manifestation of the Divine Soul, and the Divine Influence goes forth from Him. "In Him dwells all the fulness of the Godhead bodily" (Colossians 2:9), which is why He is called "the brightness of [the Father's] glory, and the express image of His person" (Hebrews 1:3).

This is not what Sabellianism teaches. The Father, the Son, and the Holy Spirit are not three manifestations of an unknown God. They are the three parts of the visible God—the Lord Jesus Christ.

Incidentally, the adherents of Judaism know the name of their God, Jehovah or Yahweh; Muslims call their God Allah; but what is the name of the God of Christianity?

To Whom Did Jesus Pray?

When we first hear that Jesus is the one and only God, we naturally wonder, "To whom was the Lord speaking when He prayed?" He certainly prayed to the Father as if to another Person. How, then, can He be the only Divine Person, the only God?

The essential point to bear in mind always is that, while on earth encompassed by the human nature derived from Mary, the Lord was not *fully* Divine. His Divine Soul (the Father) was and always had been Divine. But He also had the human part that was not Divine, the part by which He could be tempted.

Consequently, the Lord on earth had two distinctly different kinds of consciousness. When His mind was filled with Divine affections and thoughts from the Divine Soul within Him, when He was conscious of His Divinity, He spoke and acted from Divine power. He performed miracles. He spoke with authority, and not as one of the scribes. He revealed Divine wisdom, so that people were astonished at His doctrine (Matthew 7:28–29; 13:54; Mark 1:22). He revealed more and more Divine wisdom as His life on earth progressed.

But the Lord also had another kind of consciousness. He sometimes had feelings and thoughts that rose up from the merely human part that He had inherited from His mother Mary. These were limited, finite, comparatively gross. When His mind was filled with these merely human things, He felt remote from the Divine part, separate, just as we do sometimes when our minds are filled with merely natural, worldly things. When the *human* nature prevailed, the Lord was in a state of obscurity. At such times He could be tempted. He temporarily lost sight of His Divinity within. The merely human part was thinking and speaking. At times like these, the Lord prayed to "the Father" *as if* to another Person. To whom was He speaking? He was, of course, addressing His Divine part— the Divine Soul, the ever-present invisible Divinity within.

When *we* pray, we pray to the Divine Being, who is *outside* of ourselves. We visualize God as being outside of ourselves, but it was different with the Lord. *The only Divinity in existence was within Him.* It was His Soul. This was what He called upon when in the troubled, obscure state of temptation. His human part was addressing His Divine part.

In a finite way, we surely have a similar experience when in trouble or temptation. We try to summon our better self and have it help us. On the other hand, we also carry on a kind of dialogue within our own mind when our better self looks down upon and castigates our weak and vacillating lesser self. This is when we tell ourselves: "Come on now! Wake up! Get busy! Away with this mood!" In the life of the Lord on earth there were similar experiences, such as when the Divine part of the Lord comforted the struggling human part.

The fact that the Lord prayed to His own Soul, then, should not surprise us, especially when we recall the many examples in the Psalms where David—who clearly represented the Lord on earth—spoke to his inmost soul. For example, he foreshadowed exactly the state of the Lord in Gethsemane when he cried out: "Why are you cast down, O my soul? And why are you disquieted within me?" (Psalm 43:5). Psalm 22, rightly known as the Crucifixion Psalm, leaves no room for doubt that David, in his Psalms, foreshadowed the states of mind through which the Lord was to pass when He "bowed the heavens also and came down" (Psalm 18:9).

In confirmation of this Divine descent, it is a remarkable fact that after the resurrection, after even the body had been made Divine, there is no mention whatever of the Lord's praying to the Father or giving thanks to Him. There are, indeed, some places where the Father and the Son are mentioned, but this is only for the sake of describing the Divine and the human in the Lord. Only while His human part was in the process of being glorified, or made Divine, did the Lord pray to the Father *as if* to someone else. After His resurrection, however, when this process had been completed, there is no mention whatever of the Son's praying to the Father. This surely confirms the truth that the Divine and the human were then united in the Lord, so that He then had only *one* kind of consciousness. Only then could He give peace to the disciples; *peace* means "unity." Only then did He give the Holy Spirit to His disciples (John 20:21,22).

The Lord on the Cross

The explanation just given also sheds light on two other passages in the Gospels that have sometimes been advanced as objections to the new view of the trinity. These are two utterances of the Lord on the cross: "My God, My God, why have You forsaken Me?" (Matthew 27:46) and "Father, forgive them, for they do not know what they do" (Luke 23:34).

On the cross, the last of the Lord's lifelong temptations, He was painfully aware of the body to the exclusion of the Soul, as we are in a finite way during our temptations. Here the last vestiges of the human body from Mary (and its mind) were crying out in desperation to the Divine Soul within, which seemed remote, afar off. The Divine soul seemed to have forsaken the human part. "Why have You forsaken Me?"

The second passage presents a similar case—with regard to forgiveness. Forgiveness comes only from the influence of the soul, not the body. We also have to be raised above what is merely human and natural before we can forgive. Forgiveness is not a *human* characteristic, but a *Divine* one. Whenever we forgive, it is because we have received something from the Lord which prompts us to be forgiving. That is why the Lord on the cross—still speaking from the dying human part—called on the Divinity within Him (the Father) to forgive those who despitefully used Him.

The Lord's Baptism

Another passage in the Word seems to be a stumbling block as well: "And Jesus, when He had been baptized, came up immediately from the water; and behold, the heavens were opened to Him, and He saw the Spirit of God descending like a dove, and alighting on Him. And suddenly a voice came from heaven, saying, 'This is My Beloved Son, in whom I am well pleased'" (Matthew 3:16–17). To interpret this passage correctly, we need to pay close attention to what is actually being said here, rather than to what has usually been read into this incident.

Can we honestly say that we have a trinity of persons here? The three things mentioned are a Beloved Son, a dove, and a voice. We can hardly think that a dove is a person, and surely a voice is not a person. The only Person actually mentioned is the Son.

The Son means "the Divine Body," in which dwells the unseen Divine Soul and from which goes forth the Divine Influence called the Holy Spirit.

The voice heard on this occasion, then, was the voice of the Divine Soul within the Lord. It is said to be a voice from heaven, but heaven is not up in the clouds or in the sky. As the Lord Himself was to say on a later occasion: "The kingdom of God is within you" (Luke 17:21). The voice, then, came from within, from the heavenly or Divine part of the Lord, saying, "This is My Beloved Son, in whom I am well pleased"; in other words, "This is the body in which I am pleased to dwell. I have begotten it." The baptism or washing of the body represented prophetically the cleansing process by which the Lord was to make even his bodily level to become Divine, a process that was not finished until the end of His life on earth. When His bodily level had been fully glorified or made Divine, when the Lord had in this way created for Himself a *Divine* human form, He could be well pleased with it. That is why the Divine or heavenly voice coming from within said on the occasion of this representative baptism that it was well pleased with the Divine Body in which dwells all the fullness of Divinity. The baptism, representing as it did the baptism of temptation—the washing away of hereditary tendencies to evil—was a forecast of what the Lord was about to do. So there is no need to think of the voice from heaven as being that of another Person. It was the voice of the Divine Soul within.

But what about the dove? Surely we cannot think that the Spirit of God is in fact a dove, even if in Luke's Gospel it is said to have "descended in bodily form *like* a dove" (Luke 3:22). There must be a good reason for the Spirit of God to be represented by a dove, but let us not think that it *is* a dove, or that a dove is a person, Divine or otherwise. A dove is a symbol of the Spirit of God, something that represents—or re-presents—it.

What is it about a dove that makes it such a fitting representation for the Lord's Holy Spirit? When we think of a dove, we think of monogamy and of peace. A dove is well known for instinctively remaining faithful to one mate, and therefore it is an outstanding example of monogamy in mating habits. Consequently, it has become a symbol for genuine marriage love, that is, the spiritual love of *one* of the opposite sex. In addition, because of this aspect of union or unity, the dove has also become a symbol for peace, the essential idea in peace being unity rather than division, strife, or separateness.

For these reasons, a dove in the Word of God stands for truth wedded to goodness. As we all know, it is not sufficient for us just to know the truth; we also have to do what is good. "Be doers of the word, and not hearers only, deceiving your own souls" (James 1:22). The truth tells us what is good, but we must actually *do* the good thing. Then truth and goodness are wedded together; there is a union, a marriage, between what we know and what we do. A dove is what represents this union of the true and the good.

Consequently, the Holy Spirit was represented at the Lord's baptism by a dove. It was obviously meant to represent the union between the Divine and the human in the Lord, the complete oneness that was to be brought about when the human body and mind of the Lord had finally been made Divine, or glorified. This is what was forecast at the baptism, but when it was actually accomplished, the Lord became the Prince of Peace and could send forth His Holy Spirit upon the church represented by the disciples. This helps us see why it was said at one time during the Lord's life on earth, "The Holy Spirit was not yet, because Jesus was not yet glorified" (John 7:39). This is what the original actually says, not "was not yet *given*." The word *given* is written in italics, indicating that the word is not in the original. The Holy Spirit was not yet, "because Jesus was not yet glorified." But *after* even His bodily level had been made Divine, or glorified, "then Jesus said to them again, 'Peace to you! As the Father has sent Me, I also send you.' And when He had said this, He breathed on them, and said to them, 'Receive the Holy Spirit'" (John 20:21–22).

Before leaving the scene of the baptism, we should notice one more thing: The Word of God is very careful to avoid anything that might give grounds for believing that there are three persons in God. The only Person in the human form at the baptism, as we have just seen, was Jesus. The voice is not a person, nor is the dove. Surely it must be obvious that this way of describing the attributes of the Divine Being is used in order to prevent us from supposing that there are three distinct persons. If the Divine Author of the Word had wanted us to think of Him as being three persons, here, surely, was a wonderful opportunity to put it beyond doubt. Why was it not said, for example: "And God the Holy Spirit descended and hovered over Him. And God the Father looked down from heaven and said, 'This is My Beloved Son'"? If these are the ideas that are intended, why then were they not expressed? The only reason is that they are altogether opposed to the truth, the reality, that within Jesus Christ is the Divine trinity of soul, body, and emanating influence. "In Him dwells all the fulness of the Godhead bodily" (Colossians 2:9).

It is indeed a remarkable fact that whenever these three essential attributes of God are represented anywhere in the Word of God, the same care is taken not to use any symbols that might give the idea of three Divine persons. Take, for, instance, the fifth chapter of the Book of Revelation, where the subject is the human nature of the Lord—God incarnate, God in the flesh. Is this represented as another Divine Person? No, it certainly is not, because that would unquestionably have given the idea of *two* Divine Persons. To avoid doing that, to prevent us from thinking that, the appearance of a Lamb is presented, having seven horns and seven eyes. The Lamb is surely not a person; after all, what person has seven horns and seven eyes? But the Lamb represents the one God in His human form, God Incarnate. The body in which He dwells is not a separate person, any more than your body is a person separate from you. That is why care is taken not to have it represented by another person, but by a lamb, which is not a person.

Who Was Running the Universe?

Another nagging question sometimes arises in the mind of a person trying earnestly to see that Jesus is the one and only God. It is this: "If Jesus was God the Creator appearing on earth in a human form, then how was the universe governed while He was on earth with the mind of a child?"

That is a most important question that needs to be treated seriously. The answer can be stated briefly in this way: that the universe was governed by His Divine Soul, which was within, and which had *always* governed the universe. Or, as a member of my Inquirers' Class once aptly put it, "It was on automatic pilot!"

The word *soul* is used to mean many things, but what is strictly called the soul in reference to humankind is that receptacle of life that we all have—good and evil alike. Every human being, without exception, has an inmost spiritual vessel or organ receiving life from the Lord. That inmost vessel is what is called the soul. It is the first thing in us that is acted upon by the Lord and receives life from Him. But note that it is not physical. It is not to be confused with anything in the physical body; it is made of *spiritual* substance, a spiritual organ or vessel. Without it, nobody could live. Nor is it to be confused with the mind, which is an organ of consciousness. We are never conscious of our soul. Our soul is *above* our mind.

However, the Divine Soul—God's Soul—is not a receptacle of life. It is life itself, the source of all life.

But what, we may wonder, does a human soul *do?* Not only is it the part of us that, first of all, receives life from the Lord, but it is also instrumental in directing the formation of the body in the womb of a mother, as we saw in Chapter 2 when discussing the virgin birth. The operation of the soul is that mysterious force that directs the whole process of cells dividing in just the right way, according to Divine order. Life from the Divine Being flows in and is received by the soul, which channels it in order to perform various functions throughout the body. All of our involuntary or automatic functions, such as the visceral reflexes—those things in our body that work quite apart from our mind, our thinking, and our willing—are directed by the soul. It acts into and upon the rear brain, which is technically known as the cerebellum, and through that it exercises control over all the automatic, involuntary, unconscious functions of the body.

This happens even with a newborn baby, who has very little mind or consciousness at all, and it goes on through life no matter what stage of development our mind is in or what state it is in. The state of the mind has no bearing whatsoever on the soul and its action on the unconscious brain center, the soul (as just defined) being above the mind.

For example, what happens if we scratch our hand? Provided that scratch is kept clean, it will heal automatically. It is not the body, of course, that heals itself. The body, in itself, is just flesh. The action of the soul—a spiritual organism, a finite receptacle of life—is what channels life from the Lord and automatically does the healing and restores order in the body.

This kind of intuitive working of the soul goes on even when we are asleep. The state of our mind has no bearing on the soul and the involuntary or automatic functions of the body because the mind is *beneath* the soul, and action always goes from the higher to the lower, not the reverse. However, the mind can influence the voluntary functions of the body, which are controlled by the cerebrum, as in psychosomatic disorders.

Another example is growth. This is another involuntary process of the soul in the body that goes on quite apart from the thinking and willing of the mind. This is why the Lord Himself said, "Which of you by worrying can add one cubit to his stature?" (Matthew 6:27).

The same principle applies with the Divine Soul, except that the Divine Soul is not a receptacle of life but life itself. Just as our own individual soul governs the involuntary functions of our body, so the Divine Soul governed not only the body that it had created for Itself, but also the whole universe. It had *always* governed the universe. In fact, this Divine Soul had *created* the whole universe. From infinite love and wisdom, the Divine soul—known as Jehovah God—provided what was needed in the whole universe, intuitively sensing what was needed to maintain a state of order, just as our soul, on a finite scale, intuitively provides for the needs of the body.

When the Divine Soul—the inmost of Divinity—saw the need to be more closely and more personally present with humankind on the physical plane, He created a human body for Himself by means of the virgin Mary. But the fact that this human part was, in the beginning, merely human and finite or limited, the fact that it began life with only the rudiments of a mind as does every newborn baby, that in no way prevented the Divine Soul from continuing to operate as it had always done, and so rule the universe. Even when the Lord's human mind was barely conscious, even when it was asleep, the Divine Soul continued to govern the universe. After all, we are assured in the Old Testament that "He who keeps Israel shall neither slumber nor sleep" (Psalm 121:4).

It is the same with our own soul. It governs our body even while our minds are asleep. Our soul neither slumbers nor sleeps. It is a finite image of the Divine Soul.

What trips us up and causes us to stumble when considering this question is the concept of space. We easily envision heaven as being "up in the sky," as if an immense quantity of space intervened between "God in heaven" and "God Incarnate." But let us always bear in mind that the Divine Soul was not outside of the Lord on earth, but was present within Him. This is what spoke the words and did the works.

In summary, the universe was governed by the Divine Soul of Jesus, which was within and which had always governed the universe. It was in no way impeded by the mind or body of the Lord on earth. In the end, it made even these to be Divine also.

8

WHAT IS "SAVING" FAITH?

Saving faith is to believe in Him.

Emanuel Swedenborg
True Christian Religion 3:2

S aving faith is the faith that comes from charity or goodwill. Charity is essentially an outgoing attitude of mind that wishes well to others. This charitable attitude or good will is the motivating force within good deeds that makes them genuine works of charity. A good deed is a good work only if it springs from the essence of charity, wishing well to others.

Saving faith is the kind of faith that a truly charitable person has. The way charitable people believe or the kind of insight that they have is markedly different from the merely theoretical kind of faith of an uncharitable person. They know what they are talking about, from experience.

Since charity or goodwill, expressed by a life in agreement with the Divine commandments acknowledged as Divine, is what makes faith saving, we have as much of faith as we have of charity. The two go together.

The Old and New Testaments both emphasize that enlightened faith comes from a life of willing obedience to the Lord's commandments, which is a life of charity:

> A good understanding have all those who do His commandments. (Psalm 111:10)

> I understand more than the ancients because I keep Your precepts. (Psalm 119:100)

> And this is the condemnation, that the light has come into the world, and men loved darkness rather than light, because their deeds were evil. For everyone practicing evil hates the light and does not come to the light, lest his deeds should be exposed. But he who does the truth comes to the light, that his deeds may be clearly seen, that they have been done in God. (John 3:19–21; see also Matthew 12:34–35)

These Scripture passages teach in various ways that faith is a *result* of charity as defined above. They cannot be separated. This idea was well known in the early Christian Church. The Apostle John says in one of his letters:

> He who says he is in the light, and hates his brother, is in darkness even until now. He who loves his brother abides in the light, and there is no cause for stumbling in him. But he who hates his brother is in darkness and walks in darkness, and does not know where he is going, because the darkness has blinded his eyes. (1 John 2:9–11)

But *how* do goodwill and faith go together?

Faith is really goodwill manifesting itself in our thought, feelings of charity appearing to the intellect or the *sight* of the mind. So if the goodwill of charity is absent, saving faith is absent.

The human mind has two parts: the will and the understanding (or intellect). The will is the *feeling* part, consisting of affections, delights, loves, desires, lusts, passions, emotions. The understanding is the *seeing* part of the mind, consisting of thoughts, reasonings, ideas, concepts, conclusions, beliefs. Charity or goodwill is an affection we *feel* in our will. Faith comes from that affection belonging to charity, but it is *seen* in our thoughts, which belong to the other part of our mind, the intellect or understanding.

Charity and faith are like the heat and light of the sun, the one within the other. The light is a manifestation of the heat so that it can be seen. The warmth of charity cannot be seen or thought about or talked about until it presents itself in a visual form in the intellect or understanding. It is then called faith.

Yet faith may *appear* to come before charity. We may well ask ourselves: "How can charity be first? How can we have charity without faith in God? How would we know what charity is unless we had faith in the Lord's Word? Surely, we must have faith before we have charity."

But the Apostle Paul penetrates the appearance, saying: "Now abide faith, hope, and love, these three; but the greatest of these is love" (1 Corinthians 13:13). Love of one's neighbor, which is charity, is greater than faith because it is the father, the origin, of faith.

It is true that a *knowledge* of faith—of what we are supposed to believe and supposed to do—is the starting point. But that is not the same as actually believing or doing.

A knowledge of faith is only a theoretical kind of faith. It is like the theoretical understanding of recent graduates from engineering school. They have the knowledge in their heads, but they have no experience. They know what they are supposed to do, but they have not yet done it. The experienced engineers who have to train the new ones tend to smile at their theoretical formulas. They know the recent graduates do not understand them from *insight*. They will gain that insight only as they apply and use their theoretical knowledge. As they do this, it will be transformed into a *practical* knowledge, vastly different from mere theoretical knowledge. They will gradually begin to understand what they have been told by their professors in engineering school.

Acquiring a religious faith is similar. We begin with a theoretical knowledge of what the Lord's Word tells us to believe and do. We know what we are supposed to believe and do. But we begin to understand and really *believe* that knowledge only as we actually practice it. Then we believe from insight. We acknowledge what we have been taught in a new way, because now we can see why the Lord commanded it. We have moved from a merely theoretical faith to a *practical* faith—faith from charity, the faith of a charitable person. This change in the quality of faith is the first miracle—the changing of the water into wine (John 2:1–11).

We can see, then, why James said in his famous letter that "faith, by itself, if it does not have works, is dead, being alone" (James 2:17). Swedenborg also said that "no one can have faith in the Lord unless he is in charity" (The *Doctrine of Faith* 22), explaining that "the will leads the understanding and makes it act as one with itself" (*The Doctrine of Life* 44).

Charity (which is essentially an attitude of mind, a feeling of goodwill) and faith must be joined together in genuine good works; otherwise charity and faith are just mental and perishable things, like castles in the air that have no foundation.

What Does Believing Mean?

"Saving faith is to believe in *Him*," that is, in the one God, the Lord God the Savior Jesus Christ.

The Gospels say that we are to believe in the Lord Jesus Christ, that is, to "adhere to, trust, and rely on" Him (*Young's Analytical Concordance of the Bible*):

> [Jesus said,] "This is the will of Him who sent Me, that everyone who sees the Son and believes in Him may have everlasting life; and I will raise him up at the last day." (John 6:40)

Whoever believes in Him [the Son] should not perish, but have eternal life; for God so loved the world that He gave His only begotten Son, that whoever believes in Him should not perish but have everlasting life. (John 3:15–16)

He who believes in Him [the Son of God] is not condemned; but he who does not believe has been condemned already, because he has not believed in the name of the only-begotten Son of God. (John 3:18; see also John 3:36; 11:25–26; 8:24)

Numerous passages say that we are to believe in the Lord Jesus Christ as God, but they apply only to those who have the possibility of learning from the Word of God, not to people who have no access to the Word. To condemn people who have never heard of the Lord would be highly unjust.

So in the Acts of the Apostles, the Apostle Peter says to the Roman centurion Cornelius, "a devout man and one who feared God" but who knew nothing of Jesus, "I perceive that God shows no partiality: but in every nation whoever fears Him and works righteousness is accepted by Him" (Acts 10:34–35).

The scriptural selections that show the need for Christians to believe in the Divinity of Jesus point to the meaning of "to believe." It means much more than simply believing that Jesus existed as an historical character. To believe in Jesus is to believe in Him as Divine, as God, as having Divine power. That is why He always asked those whom He was about to heal, "Do you believe that I am able to do this?" (Matthew 9:28; Mark 9:23). After performing the healing, Jesus would say, "According to your faith let it be to you" (see Matthew 9:28–30).

Two other passages from the Gospel of Matthew provide even more clarification:

And when He had come to His own country, He taught them in their synagogue, so that they were astonished and said, "Where did this Man get this wisdom and these mighty works? Is this not the carpenter's son? Is not His mother called Mary? And His brothers James, Joseph, Simon, and Judas? And his sisters, are they not all with us? Where then did this Man get all these things?" So they were offended at Him. But Jesus said to them, "A prophet is not without honor except in his own country and in his own house." And He did not do many mighty works there because of their unbelief. (Matthew 13:54–58)

"His own country" is where Jesus grew up: Nazareth in Galilee. The people there found great difficulty in believing that Jesus was in any sense Divine. He was too familiar to them. They had seen Him grow up, and they knew His family, His brothers and sisters. They were too close to His human part to see His Divinity. As a consequence, He could not do many marvelous works in Nazareth because of their unbelief, because of their denial of His Divinity.

But to believe in His Divinity—that is from heaven; that is "to believe in Him." The second passage in Matthew says the same thing:

He said to them, "But who do you say that I am?" And Simon Peter answered and said, "You are the Christ, the Son of the living God." And Jesus answered and said to him, "Blessed are you, Simon Bar-Jona, for flesh and blood has not revealed this to you, but My Father who is in heaven. And I also say to you that you are Peter, and on this rock I will build My church and the gates of Hades shall not prevail against it. And I will give you the keys of the kingdom of heaven, and whatever you bind on earth will be bound in heaven, and whatever you loose on earth will be loosed in heaven." (Matthew 16:15–19)

"But who do you say that I am?" The Lord asks not only His disciples of old but every one of us that question, through the ages.

The Greek word for *Peter* is *Petros,* while the word for *rock* or *foundation-stone* is *petra,* a different word. So it is a manifest mistake to identify the man Peter as the rock, which is sometimes done. It is what Peter *said* that is the rock or foundation-stone of the church: his confession of faith, his belief or acknowledgment that the Lord was the promised Messiah, God in human form, "the Son," meaning the human form of the living God. In other words, He *acknowledged* Jesus' Divinity. That is the rock on which the church is founded, and the key that opens heaven, if you believe it from the heart. Denial of it closes heaven because the Lord Jesus Christ is the God of heaven and earth.

Believing in Jesus could not mean believing that He suffered on the cross and took the punishment for our sins. The crucifixion had not yet taken place at the time of the two incidents reported in Matthew. Other passages show that without an acknowledgment of His Divinity, the Lord could not work miracles. That is why, before performing any miracle, Jesus usually asked whether the patient believed in His Divine power or not. It would make no sense for Jesus to ask whether the person believed, *before* the event, that by His death He took away the punishment due to sin. But it makes eminent sense to think that He was asking whether the person about to be healed believed in His Divine power, His ability to heal and save. If the person suffering could say from the heart, "Heal me, O Lord, and I shall be healed; save me, and I shall be saved. For You are my praise" (Jeremiah 17:14), if he or she believed that Jesus had almighty power, then Jesus could work a miracle, but not otherwise.

Why Believe in Jesus?

Why must we believe in *Jesus?* Why not believe in the Father? Why is such emphasis placed on believing in the Son?

Swedenborg gives this very interesting answer: "Men ought to believe, that is, have faith, in God the Savior Jesus Christ, because that is a faith in a visible God within whom is what is invisible" (*True Christian Religion* 339).

The Lord Jesus Christ is God *visible*, in whom is the invisible Divine Soul. At one time, God was visible to the physical senses—the eyes and ears of men, women, and children who actually sensated Him. And the Lord is still visible to us today, in a certain sense. We can have an image of the Lord in our minds; we can visualize or see Him in our mind's eye. As we read the Gospels, a picture forms in our mind of Jesus in the boat, walking on the water, praying on the mountain, breaking bread, healing people, teaching people, and so on. At the very least, we have an image of a person in human form. As we read about the Transfiguration, when Jesus went up into a mountain with three of the disciples and was transfigured before them, we form a picture of a Divine Man, the Lord in all His glory, with face shining and garments a brilliant white (Matthew 17:1–8; Mark 9:2–8; Luke 9:28–36). With their spiritual eyes and ears opened, the three disciples saw the Lord as visible in heaven. That was a prophecy of the way the Lord was to appear after being resurrected: no longer the *crucified* Lord but the *risen* Lord, the *Divine* Human, the one and only object of worship.

The Gospels show that believing in the Father alone is a belief in what is invisible: "You have neither heard His voice at any time, nor seen His form" (John 5:37). The Divine Soul as it is in itself—referred to as "the Father" here—will always be invisible, just as our human soul is invisible, except insofar as our mind and body reveal it. "No one has seen God at any time. The only begotten Son who is in the bosom of the Father, He has declared Him" (John 1:18). All that we could ever know of the Divine Soul has been revealed by the Divine Body, God Incarnate.

Why is the Lord here and elsewhere called the *only begotten* Son? In the King James translation of the New Testament, one passage calls people who accept the Lord "sons of God" (see John 1:12), causing some people to say, "Oh, yes, Jesus is the Son of God, but so is everybody else who accepts Him." However, they have overlooked the term *the only begotten,* which occurs in several places (John 1:14, 18; 3:16–18). There was something unique or special about the human form that God put on in order to be more present with people on earth. In the French language, Jesus is called *le Fils unique* (the unique Son). His human form was unique because Divinity dwelt within it in fullness, something no one else could claim.

John 14:9–10 reveals that the Father, or the Divine Soul, dwells within. Being invisible, it dwells within the *visible* God. That is what was unique about this particular human form; God Himself dwelt within it. He was its very Soul. No human being can claim that. The most we can ever claim is that we are receiving life from the Lord into our souls, but the Soul of the Lord Jesus Christ was Divine; it was God. He was "the only begotten" not only because God was His Soul and His Soul was God, but also because this was the *only* time God had appeared in His own human form, and the only time He ever will. No prophecy of His second coming ever says that He will be born of woman again, the only way of becoming physically present on earth.

The Importance of "God Visible"

It is very important to be able to visualize the God you are praying to, the God you worship. Many sincere Christians find themselves at some point wondering whom they should worship or pray to. This is especially true when young people reach age fifteen or sixteen and begin to think about the things they have been taught, trying to understand them.

But when we realize that in Jesus Christ dwells all the fullness of the Godhead in bodily form (Colossians 2:9), we can visualize the Lord Jesus Christ. We have an object of worship, Someone on whom our mind can focus its sight. That is why it is so important to have this concept of a *visible* God.

We can believe in, worship, and pray to a visible God. We cannot address an invisible God, one that we cannot visualize. That is quite impossible. Nor can we pray to an abstraction such as Divine love, Divine wisdom, or any other abstract Divine quality. Could we have a conversation with Divine love and Divine wisdom?

As our common sense tells us, that is quite impossible. If we picture God as a force or a spirit (if by that we mean something formless), it is likewise impossible to be on speaking terms with Him. We cannot talk to a force. We cannot worship a force. We might be able to talk *about* it, but it is only when we see the Divine qualities embodied in a Divine Person that our mind has an object to focus upon.

The idea of "God-Man" can be seen in thought, and so it can summon the presence of the Divine Being. The law of the mind and of the spiritual world is that "thought brings presence." If the idea of God is not focused upon some Divine Person whom we can visualize and whom we can consequently approach, then it is indeterminate, and therefore hazy. On the other hand, faith in God-Man "has an object from which and to which it goes forth, and when once it is received, it is permanent, as when anyone has seen an emperor or king, as often as the fact is recalled the image returns" (*True Christian Religion* 339:3).

Once, when we were talking about this topic in one of my Inquirers' Classes, a woman who had been paying rapt attention spoke up eagerly, saying: "I am so glad we are discussing this. Before I found the New Church, there seemed to be God up there somewhere—doing nothing—and Jesus was down here. *And I could never get the two together.*"

That, of course, is the whole point: getting the two together. We must keep soul and body together—the inner essence *and* the outer form or manifestation, the two together. In fact, it could truly be said that the two together applies in any subject we look at in the new view of Christianity: God, the Word of God, heaven, marriage, the life of charity, or faith. In every case, we must have the internal and the external, the soul and the body together. And we need to have a balance between the two. If we overemphasize the internal at the expense of the external—the soul at the expense of the body—it is like a castle in the air; it has no basis. If we focus only on the external, there is no spirituality in it. So that is the grand theme that runs throughout the whole of the New Christianity: keeping soul and body together. For that reason, we have been emphasizing the need to have "faith in a visible God within whom is what is invisible." That is why we must "believe in *Him*"—in the Lord God Jesus Christ, Creator and Redeemer.

Other Kinds of Faith

Saving faith is the only kind that is spiritual in quality, that is, the only one that comes from a spiritual origin. It comes from the spiritual or supraconscious level of our mind, which is heavenly. All other kinds of faith, being destitute of that spiritual essence, are merely natural in quality.

One example is historical faith or the faith of authority, sometimes called heritage faith. We all begin with that type of faith, believing what our church teaches from the authority of others whom we admire and respect. We believe what they say, not because we have seen the truth of it, but simply because those people seem to be authorities who know much more than we do. Historical faith is essentially no different from our faith in history. We believe, for instance, that Julius Caesar existed, not because we have ever met him or read any of the documents concerning him, but simply because we have faith in the writers of history books and in history teachers. Our faith in matters of religion can be little different from our faith in history. In the beginning, we really do not have a faith of our own because we do not have a *sight* of our own. We have someone else's faith grafted onto us. There is no spiritual essence in that kind of faith; it is merely natural, based on personality. It has penetrated no further than the memory. It may not even have reached our understanding, but remains a memorized faith, mere persuasion.

The difference between that kind of faith and a real personal conviction is graphically illustrated in the joyous exclamations of the Samaritan men upon hearing the Lord Himself, after having been told about Him by the Samaritan woman who had met Him at Jacob's well. "And many more believed because of His own word. Then they said to the woman, 'Now we believe, not because of what you said, for we have heard for ourselves and know that this is indeed the Christ, the Savior of the world'" (John 4:41–42).

Then there is faith in an invisible God, a belief in God as something other than a Divine Person, a formless spirit perhaps, something like a breath of wind or a force. This kind of faith most often arises from a denial of the Lord's Divinity.

Another kind of natural faith is a belief in a trinity of Divine Persons, which in the final analysis is a belief in three gods, the denials of its proponents notwithstanding. Their protests are quite understandable, because they know that believing in more gods than one is polytheism. The advocates of "God in three Persons, Blessed Trinity" would no doubt be alarmed and hurt if they could see the logical consequence of that doctrine. But they are preserved from that experience by the claim, frankly admitted on all sides, that the idea of God as taught in the orthodox Christian Church is a mystery; so God is invisible. The doctrine of this trinity cannot enter into the thought. People can say it, but they cannot *think* it. Yet if there is no thought, there can be no presence. Thought brings presence, and the presence of the Lord can lead to being joined with Him, and therefore to salvation. "Saving faith is to believe in *Him*."

The Mechanics of Belief

There are two requirements for a faith that keeps soul and body together: light and knowledge (or a true idea of the Lord). The light of faith must come from above. This also is clear from the Gospels:

> Jesus answered and said to him, "Most assuredly, I say to you, unless one is born again, he cannot see the kingdom of God." (John 3:3)

John answered and said, "A man can receive nothing unless it has been given to him from heaven." (John 3:27)

Then they said to Him, "What shall we do, that we might work the works of God?" Jesus answered and said to them, "This is the work of God, that you believe in Him whom He has sent." (John 6:28–29)

Belief in the Divinity of the Lord is the work of God. God put that light into our mind, into the higher or inmost part of our mind—everyone's mind. So that part of the process of believing in the Lord is entirely His work. As we saw earlier, "it is the Divine that bears witness concerning the Divine, and not man from himself" (*Apocalypse Explained* 635:2). So we need to be looking to the Lord and working in conjunction with Him in order to have a spiritual kind of faith, "a faith in a visible God within whom is what is invisible."

There are two levels of our mind: the heavenly or spiritual mind and the earthly or natural (conscious) mind. "In the beginning God created the heavens and the earth" (Genesis 1:1). There is a part of our mind that is above our conscious awareness: our supraconscious mind. We think *from* that mind, but not *in* it; and that heavenly or spiritual part of our mind is always in a state of order, always enlightened by the Lord. Only our earthly, conscious mind is ever out of order. The whole purpose of our life on earth is to cooperate with the Lord in bringing our natural mind back into order so that heavenly feelings and thoughts can flow in.

"Faith in its essence is spiritual, but in its form it is natural" (*True Christian Religion* 339). In other words, the light of faith is of a spiritual quality; it comes from above our conscious awareness. It comes from the spiritual level of our mind, having been put there by the Lord. This applies to every human mind, without exception. An earlier teaching in *True Christian Religion* says, "There is a universal influx from God into the souls of men of the truth that there is a God, and that He is one" (*True Christian Religion* 8).

This being the case, we naturally ask how it is possible for people to be atheists, denying God. If everyone receives this light, why doesn't everyone believe in some kind of God, especially in God-Man?

There are two reasons for this. One is that our natural mind may be so tightly closed against the spiritual mind that it blocks out that universal influx. Everyone receives that inflow of light in the higher or heavenly mind, but not everyone receives it in the lower or natural mind. Evils of life and thought in that lower mind impose a mindset that focuses our sight entirely on natural things, so that it reacts against *anything* from above. The spiritual mind is then closed off.

The other reason for denying God is a lack of knowledge. Unless the spiritual light that causes faith falls upon some ideas about God in our natural, conscious mind, we will not be enlightened. If there is nothing in our mind to reflect that light, we do not see it.

Having a light come on in our mind is a common experience for us in this world. We experience that flash of light when at last we understand what another person is saying—perhaps in a mathematics or physics class, or when reading a legal agreement or tax instructions. In our cloudy mind we grasp, at first, only words, words, words. But suddenly we catch the *idea* behind the words, and the light comes on.

This is similar to seeing the spiritual light that causes faith in God and heaven. That light needs to fall on some distinct idea or ideas about spiritual realities in order to be reflected back and enlighten them.

But these ideas of the Lord need to be true, drawn accurately from the Word of God, from what the Lord Himself has revealed about Himself in a written, objective Divine revelation. In the proportion that our ideas of the Lord are distorted by evil loves or twisted by false reasonings and mistaken concepts, those ideas cannot serve adequately as suitable receptacles for the inflow of the light that causes faith. That is why not everybody has this belief in God. But where the two requirements are present in our conscious mind—spiritual light (the essence of faith) and true ideas (the forms of faith)—then the universal inflow from the Lord is received and a spiritual kind of faith results. Then, like the man in the Gospels who had been born blind and whose eyes the Lord opened, we exclaim, "One thing I know: that though I was blind, now I see" (John 9:25).

Since faith is a spiritual kind of seeing, it is analogous to physical sight. In order for us to see anything with our bodily eyesight, we need light and we need an object to be seen, as well as an organ of sight.

There is such a thing as having too much light, which blinds us. If, for example, we look at a snow-covered landscape that is bathed in bright sunlight, we see absolutely nothing. There is too much light. But if only one tree is visible, or one person, or any object at all, the light is reflected back from that object, and for the first time, we see something.

The process is identical with spiritual sight, or faith. We need light from above, an object on which the light may fall, and an organ of sight—our intellect or understanding. Only when these three are present do we have genuine faith. We become aware of the light only when it falls on some idea that we have in our conscious mind. The light of faith is spiritual, but it must be formulated; it must take form by falling upon a true idea in our conscious mind. Otherwise, it does not produce that sight of the truth we call faith or genuine belief.

Swedenborg summarizes the matter like this:

> People ought to believe, that is, have faith, in God the Savior Jesus Christ, because that is a faith in a visible God within whom is what is invisible; and faith in a visible God, who is at once Man and God enters into a person; for faith in its essence is spiritual but in its form it is natural; consequently with mankind such a faith becomes spiritual-natural. For anything spiritual, in order to

be anything with man, must have a receptacle in the natural.
(*True Christian Religion* 339)

The passage then goes on to ask a very pertinent question:

> What is faith without an object on which it is focussed? Is it not
> like gazing into the universe, where the sight falls, as it were, into
> vacuity and is lost? . . . In a word, faith in an invisible God is actu-
> ally blind, since the human mind fails to see its God; and the light
> of that faith, not being spiritual-natural faith, is a fatuous light,
> which light is like that of the glow-worm. (*True Christian Religion*
> 339)

In the original Latin in which Swedenborg wrote, there are
two words for light: *lux* and *lumen. Lux* means bright sunlight.
Lumen is a luminous, phosphorescent light that must be sur-
rounded by darkness to be seen at all. *Lumen* is the word used for
the "glow-worm" light in the passage quoted.

The consequences of trying to see in that light are then
noted:

> From that light nothing comes except what pertains to fantasy,
> which creates a belief that the apparent is the real when yet it is
> not. Faith in an invisible God shines with no other light than this,
> especially when God is thought to be a Spirit, and spirit is
> thought to be like ether. What follows but that man regards God
> as he does the ether? Consequently he seeks God in the universe;
> and when he does not find Him there, he believes the nature of
> the universe to be God. This is the origin of the prevailing natu-
> ralism of the day. (*True Christian Religion* 339)

This naturalism started with a belief in an invisible God—a
formless God, invisible like ether. If God is invisible, humankind inevitably turns to nature as the ruling force. What alternative is
there? How else can this end but in naturalism—the idea that nature determines everything, a belief in Mother Nature instead of in
Father God?

Denying the Divinity of the Lord Jesus Christ destroys the object in the mind that should catch and receive the light: the image of the Lord as the Divine Human, the visible God. When that idea is absent, the light simply passes through and is "not received." In that case, faith is merely natural, "destitute of a spiritual essence," mere "persuasion" (*True Christian Religion* 339).

We Are Meant to Understand

If it is true that we need to have an accurate knowledge of the Lord derived from His Word, it is equally true that we need that light from the spiritual level of our mind. We are meant to have an enlightened faith, a faith *through understanding*. Otherwise, why would the Lord have made the following statements?

"Come now, and let us reason together," says the Lord. (Isaiah 1:18)

Let him who glories glory in this, that he understands and knows Me. (Jeremiah 9:24)

When the disciples asked Jesus why He spoke to the multitude in parables, He answered and said to them, "Because it has been given to you to know the mysteries of the kingdom of heaven, but to them it is not given. . . . When anyone hears the word of the kingdom, and does not understand it, then the wicked one comes and snatches away what was sown in his heart. This is he who received seed by the wayside." (Matthew 13:11, 19)

These things I have spoken to you in figurative language; but the time is coming when I will no longer speak to you in figurative language, but I will tell you plainly about the Father. (John 16:25)

We could draw the same conclusion from the fact that the Lord on earth condemned the Pharisees as "blind leaders of the blind" (Matthew 15:14), and chided the Samaritans with the words,

"You worship what you do not know: we know what we worship" (John 4:22).

From these Scripture passages, it is clear that a blind faith, a faith in which we declare that we believe something that we do not understand, is the opposite of "saving faith." If any religious leaders succeed in inducing us to believe whatever they say—even if we do not understand it—they can lead us wherever they wish, into a thousand quagmires of doctrine, or even to mass suicide. This actually happened in the case of Jim Jones and his followers.

How Is Saving Faith Acquired?

Saving faith is acquired by shunning our evils because they are sins against the Lord. No other motive will suffice. If we shun our evils *as sins*, we are looking to the Lord. We are inviting Him to come into our life. From Him we receive the goodness of charitable feelings. The Lord is the only source of such feelings. We receive them from Him in the same proportion as we turn our backs on whatever evil feelings we find in ourselves, and shun them as sins against Him. Every single one of those evil feelings is the opposite of some good feeling of charity.

> Just insofar as a person shuns evils as sins, just so far he has faith, because just so far is he in the goodness of charity. (*The Doctrine of Life* 45)

> Charity joins itself to faith with a man when he wills what he knows and perceives. Willing belongs to charity: knowing and perceiving belong to faith. Faith enters into a man and becomes his, when he wills and loves what he knows and perceives; till then, it is outside of him. (*The New Jerusalem and Its Heavenly Doctrine* 110)

With charity comes the light of faith. The two are together in our supraconscious mind. The extent to which we shun our evils as sins is the extent—no more and no less—to which we open our conscious mind to receive the warmth of charity and the light of faith that flow in from our heavenly or supraconscious mind. The extent to which we fail to shun our evils as sins is the extent to which our mind is closed against feelings of charity and their offspring—the light of faith—which cause us to say from the heart, "Lord, I believe" (Mark 9:24). If we want the Lord to help our unbelief, shunning our evils as sins against Him is indispensable.

The whole subject is summed up in Swedenborg's beautiful passage:

> If anyone should think within himself, or say to someone else, "Who is able to have the internal acknowledgment of truth that is faith? Not I," let me tell him how he may have it: Shun evils as sins, and come to the Lord, and you will have as much of it as you desire. (*Doctrine of Faith* 12)

So there are actually three things that are necessary for acquiring saving faith: (1) to look to the Lord Jesus Christ and believe in Him as Divine, the Divine Being; (2) to learn truths from His Divine Word; and (3) to live according to them.

It is, of course, possible for these three things to be separated, but in that case there is no *saving* faith. "Saving faith arises when the three are conjoined and becomes such as is the conjunction" (*True Christian Religion* 348).

Fluctuating Faith

The need for this conjunction explains why our faith fluctuates. Sometimes we have great faith, at other times a weak and wavering faith. For example, "The apostles said to the Lord, 'Increase our faith'" (Luke 17:5). They realized that their faith *could* be increased, that it was not something static. Likewise, the father of the child who had a deaf and dumb spirit, when asked by the Lord whether he believed, cried out and said with tears, "Lord, I believe; help my unbelief" (Mark 9:23–24). To the woman of Canaan who begged the Lord to heal her daughter, He said, "O woman, great is your faith!" (Matthew 15:28). He gave a similar testimony to the fact that we may have more or less faith when He praised the Roman centurion who believed that the Lord had only to say a word and his servant would be healed, saying to the people, "I say to you, I have not found such great faith, not even in Israel" (Luke 7:9). Yet He upbraided the disciples after calming the storm, asking them, "Why are you so fearful? How is it that you have no faith?" (Mark 4:40). As He saved the fearful Peter from drowning, He said to him, "O you of little faith, why did you doubt?" (Matthew 14:31).

There are, indeed, degrees of faith. Faith can fluctuate according to the presence or absence of the three requirements of a saving faith: looking to the Lord, learning truths from His Word, and living according to them. This is brought out in several of the Lord's parables, notably that of the wise man who built his house upon a rock:

> Therefore whoever hears these sayings of Mine, and does them, I will liken him to a wise man who built his house on the rock.... Now everyone who hears these sayings of Mine, and does not do them, will be like a foolish man who built his house on the sand. (Matthew 7:24–27)

A similar case is presented in the parable of the wise and foolish virgins. They were wise if they obeyed the commandments and foolish if they did not. The good oil of charity kept the flame of truth and faith alight. But if they lacked the oil of a life of charity, they were in the dark.

Some think that faith comes all in a rush on one great and glorious day, that you either have faith or you do not. But as a little reflection will tell us, faith fluctuates. The reason for this is that the three requirements for a saving faith must all be present. "Saving faith is to believe in Him."

The Importance of Faith

The importance of faith from charity can hardly be overstressed. This spiritual kind of faith is the means of salvation, the key to heaven. It is what opens or closes heaven. This is the meaning of the "keys of the kingdom" promised to Simon Peter when, from above, he acknowledged the Divinity of Jesus (Matthew 16:19).

Faith is not something instantaneous. It does not come at once. Faith is progressive. It grows as charity grows. We have no more of faith (spiritual or saving faith) than we have of charity. "He who does the truth comes to the light" (John 3:21).

9

EVILS AS SINS

Evils should not be done, because they belong to the devil and are from the devil.

Emanuel Swedenborg
True Christian Religion 3:2

What Are Evils?

Obviously, the question "What are evils?" is vitally important. Evils include the evil actions forbidden in the Ten Commandments (Exodus 20)—such as murder, adultery, stealing, and bearing false witness—evils that are not to be done. But more is meant by *evils* than simply evil actions.

For example, the evil of covetousness or lusting after what is evil is included in the Ten Commandments. Covetousness is the infamous soul and cause of the evil actions forbidden, which leads to murder, to adultery, to theft, and to false witness, the cover-up of evil or a defender and protector of self.

The biblical story of David and Bathsheba, Uriah's wife (2 Sam. 11), exemplifies covetousness. David lusted after Bathsheba. He coveted her. This covetousness led to adultery and Bathsheba's pregnancy. In an attempt to cover up the adultery (that is, to bear false witness), David brought Uriah home from the battlefield, hoping that he would have sexual relations with his wife, so that the child to be born would be regarded as his. When Uriah, out of loyalty to his men still suffering the rigors of the battlefield, refused the comfort of lodging in his own home, David had to change his plans. His covetousness had already led to adultery; now it led to the desire to steal away Bathsheba permanently from her husband. In order to accomplish this theft, he had first to murder Uriah. This he did deceitfully by having him placed in the forefront of the battle, so that he was consequently killed in action. In this chain of events, we see an illustration of how covetousness can lead to adultery, theft, murder, and false witness (to hide the evil).

Covetousness is a feeling, a continual wishing for the goods of others for oneself. *Selfishness* fathers covetousness; in fact, all evils come from the two loves of hell: the loves of self and of the world as predominant loves. In the case of David and Bathsheba, we can see that the love of self was within David's covetousness or lusting. The love of self produces covetousness, and covetousness, as we have seen, leads to all the evil actions forbidden in the Ten Commandments.

Selfishness—and a complete disregard for the feelings of others—lurks within all evil actions. The murderer is not concerned for the welfare of his victim; the adulterer is impervious to the misery of the aggrieved partner; the thief laughs at the plight of his victim; and the false witness is completely callous about the ruined life and character of the person whom he defamed.

Other evil feelings flowing forth from the love of self are listed in Swedenborg's *The New Jerusalem and Its Heavenly Doctrine* 75:

> The evils of those in the love of self are, in general, contempt for others, envy, enmity against those who do not show them favor,

and from that hostility towards them, hatreds of various kinds, acts of revenge, acts of cunning and deceit, mercilessness and cruelty; and where there are evils of this kind, there is also contempt for the Divine [Being], and for Divine things— the good things and true things of the Church.

Those general evils are really manifestations or symptoms of the love of self. Similarly, the love of the world manifests itself in various forms, as set out in *Heaven and Hell* 565:

There is the love of wealth for the sake of being exalted to honors, when these alone are loved. There is the love of honors and dignities with a view to the increase of wealth. There is the love of wealth for the sake of various activities that give delight in the world. There is the love of wealth merely for the sake of wealth, which is a miser's love; and so on.

So the love of the world exists in varying degrees, involving the lust of covetousness and envy, which in turn leads to the lust of possessing, which, if not curbed, can lead to dishonesty, deceit, fraud, theft, and even robbery. The worst form of the love of the world is avarice, the love of money for the sake of money.

In fact, all evil feelings and actions come forth from the two loves that rule in hell: love of self and love of the world, all contained within the outwardly evil actions forbidden in the Ten Commandments.

There are three layers of meaning in each of the commandments: (1) the literal or obvious meaning, referring to harm done to our life in this world; (2) a layer of meaning referring to our life in the spiritual world to eternity, or the Lord's kingdom rather than the kingdoms of this world; and (3) our attitude to the Lord, which is the inmost level of meaning in the Ten Commandments.

Murder

The commandment "You shall not murder"(*Exodus* 20:13) actually says *murder*. It does not say simply, "You shall not *kill*," although that is the usual, though inaccurate, translation of the original. In both the Hebrew of the Old Testament and in the Greek of the New Testament, several words mean "to kill," "to slay," or "to put to death." But one word is reserved for *murder*—the word used here, meaning "to kill from hatred." Hatred is what leads to murder. And the root of hatred is the love of ruling over everybody. Anyone who stands in the way then becomes an object of hatred, of murderous hatred. An endeavor or effort to murder lurks within hatred.

The Lord even connected anger with murder in the Sermon on the Mount: "You have heard that it was said to those of old, 'You shall not murder,' and whoever murders will be in danger of the judgment. But I say to you that whoever is angry with his brother without a cause shall be in danger of the judgment. And whoever says to his brother, '*Raca!*' shall be in danger of the council. But whoever says, 'You fool!' shall be in danger of hell fire" (Matthew 5:21,22).

Anger, contempt, and other forms of hatred are to be included in the idea of murder because these evil feelings are the *cause* of murder. Murder in intention is still murder, even though the murderous intent does not always issue forth into action. Hatred, coming from hell, spawns cruelty and a total disregard for the welfare of others. So in addition to actual murder, violence, or maiming someone's body, we must include in murder such burning passions as hatred, anger, enmity, cruelty, and revenge, together with smoldering resentment. All these evil passions are murderous in intention. Murder lies concealed in them like fire in wood underneath the ashes (*The Divine Providence* 278:5). As we have seen in an earlier chapter, "hellfire" is nothing else than those fires within us, also meant by such expressions as "inflamed with hatred," "burning with revenge," "kindling anger." All the manifestations of "hellfire" are to be included in the term *murder* because these fierce and fiery emotions are the cause of every vindictive crime of violence and murder.

The literal or obvious meaning of this commandment extends to other means of destroying a person's life in this world, such as slander and social ostracism. Slander is using vicious gossip to ruin a person's good name, to murder his or her usefulness, to belittle any good that he or she does. Assassinating a person's character is nothing other than murder. Many a good person has been stabbed in the back and done to death by malicious, vindictive slander. For most people, to lose their good name, their honor, and their self-respect is to lose their very life. Once they are slandered, their life in the world is (at the very least) maimed, so that they live a miserable existence. To take away a person's happiness in this way is tantamount to murder.

A similar form of murder sometimes practiced even today—in an age when we are supposed to be enlightened—is social ostracism. Ostracized people are cut off from society; their associates refuse to speak to them, answer them, or have anything to do with them. This cruel form of murder is a heartless manifestation of the love of self, the love of dominion, and the love of the world, and it makes a person's life miserable. He would be, as Swedenborg so tellingly put it, "living in society as one dead, for he would be numbered among the vile and wicked, with whom no one would associate. When this is done from enmity, from hatred, or from revenge, it is murder" (*The Apocalypse Explained* 1012:3).

Murdering Spiritual Life

The essential idea in the literal or obvious meaning of this commandment is the destruction of a person's life in *this* world, or making it intolerable. But we are created for another life: our life in heaven, which is *eternal* life. This does not mean the same thing as existing forever in the spiritual world, because everyone without exception is granted that. But not everyone is granted eternal life: the life of heaven, which is *spiritual* life, the only kind of life that contains eternal blessedness within it. To deprive a person of spiritual life is a more interior form of murder than destroying a person's life on earth. It is murdering someone's *soul*, which has consequences to *eternity* for the victim. So the Lord said, "Do not fear those who kill the body but cannot kill the soul. But rather fear him who is able to destroy both soul and body in hell" (Matthew 10:28). In this verse the word *soul* means a person's spiritual life. It does not refer to the spiritual organ receiving life, as defined earlier. That can never be destroyed.

How do we destroy someone's *spiritual life*, or our own, for that matter? The consistent teaching of the Word of God is that the only way people can save their soul from spiritual death (damnation) is by living in accordance with the Lord's commandments. If people are not obedient, they consequently do not believe in the Lord and become dead to all spiritual things. Being unresponsive to the Lord, they are *spiritually* dead, however lively they may otherwise be. The life of religion—the life that the commandments indicate—is the yardstick. So the Lord said, "If you want to enter into life, keep the commandments" (Matthew 19:17). *Life* obviously means eternal life, heavenly life.

Consequently, any influence that turns us away from living a spiritual life—anything that discourages us from examining ourselves or gives a false sense of security in spiritual matters—is murderous. It destroys people's spiritual lives, killing their souls, and depriving them of the life of heaven.

Many people and many forces are at work, striving with all their might to destroy charity and faith in others. As spiritual murderers, they are acting under the influence of hell, which is the great murderer. Their methods are many and various, such as ridiculing any ideas about the holiness of the Word or the Divinity of the Lord Jesus Christ, or the possibility of being truly altruistic and charitable. Spiritual murderers seduce people into believing that there is no life after death, and so they undermine the very basis of religion. Because they have contempt for everything associated with the religious way of life, they jeer at a sincere person's scruples of conscience, sneer at his or her sincerity and honesty, encouraging people to act against their conscience, and assure them that they would never be found out. Such are spiritual murderers!

We may think that we would never commit such gross spiritual murder against our fellow human beings. Yet we can unwittingly take away a person's spiritual life by destroying feelings of charity. If we act in a way that stirs up the *worst* in others; if we speak our mind regardless of the effect on the feelings of others; if we belittle people, speak contemptuously to them, disparage their works, or invite others to laugh at them, are we not provoking their worst characteristics? Are we not stirring up the weaknesses of their merely human nature, inciting their feelings of anger and resentment? Surely that destroys their feelings of charity and kills goodwill toward the neighbor.

If we realize that provoking anger in others is a very effective way of destroying their spiritual lives, we realize at the same time that we have a very great responsibility in our dealings with others. Even what may seem like petty evils are to be shunned as sins against the *spiritual* meaning of the commandment against murder.

We can destroy our own spiritual life—our own soul—too. There is such a thing as *spiritual* suicide. We help to murder our own spiritual life every time we succumb to the influences of hell, every time we allow hatred and the love of dominion—the loves of hell—to rule our words and actions. Each time we ignore the Lord's commandment "You shall not murder," we are to some extent destroying our own heavenly life, which, after all, is the only thing that makes us *truly* human.

Inmost Murder

The inmost or celestial meaning of these commandments always refers to the Lord. *Murder* in this sense means being habitually angry and resentful against the Lord, bearing hatred against Him and wishing to blot out His very name. No higher degree of murder than this exists. The Divine Being is life itself, the source of all life. Murder means destroying life—natural life, natural happiness, moral life, and spiritual life—all God's work. He is the source. To wish to destroy the source of life is the highest degree of murder. It is the inmost soul of every other kind of murder. Those who love themselves so much that they hate to hear mention of the Lord's name—those who have in this way obliterated the Lord from their mind—will have no qualms about trying to destroy another person's spiritual life by deriding the life of religion. They will delight in being openly contemptuous of it, and will rejoice when they see a disciple of the Lord waver and fall. Nor will they feel obliged to restrain their outbursts of anger against those who do not agree with them or bow down to them. They will also believe with all their heart that revenge is indeed sweet. The next step is social injury, and then bodily injury; the final step is actual murder. In that final step, all the preceding steps are contained. So we should all understand very clearly what the consequences are of obliterating the Lord from our mind. We are blotting out life in all its degrees. All these forms of murder form a unit; they lie one within the other in a coherent whole.

Adultery

It is the same with adultery. In the Sermon on the Mount, the Lord made it abundantly clear that adultery as mentioned in the commandments is not limited to the physical plane. He filled that commandment with a deeper meaning, showing that a man who looks on a woman to lust for her has committed adultery with her already in his heart (Matthew 5:28). Adultery in intention is really the same as adultery in fact—especially if it is thought to be allowable. The *will* is the person. So the Lord advises us to beware of what we entertain in our imagination. Adultery includes thinking and speaking about anything lascivious, obscene or pornographic: all off-color jokes about marriage or parts and functions of the body.

Spiritual Adultery

There is a deeper kind of adultery, just as there is a deeper kind of marriage, a marriage that refers to the Lord's kingdom, to the joining of the two parts of a person's mind—the will and the intellect—so that they are no longer two but one. The will and the understanding are wedded together when we do what the Word says is true and good. Then there is a marriage of deed and creed. All in heaven are in this *heavenly* marriage. With them there is no such thing as understanding that something is right, and doing *something else.* That would seem to them like committing adultery—turning aside from what the Lord has revealed, turning to something else.

This more interior kind of adultery takes the form of being unfaithful to the Lord's commandments as revealed in His Word, playing the harlot with His Word. Spiritual adultery is turning aside from the Bridegroom and Husband of the Church, turning to *something else*—our own wishes and inclinations. This adulteration of the good things of the Word and the falsification of its truths in the Church of their day was loudly lamented by the prophets: "They have done disgraceful things in Israel, and have committed adultery with their neighbors' wives, and have spoken lying words in My name" (Jeremiah 29:23). "They shall commit harlotry . . . because they have ceased obeying the Lord" (Hosea 4:10).

The Lord, when on earth, called the leaders of the Church "an adulterous generation" (Matthew 12:39), not because they were necessarily committing physical adultery, but because they had falsified the Word, turning away from its teachings to follow the traditions of men. This turning away from the Divine Word is a spiritual form of adultery that destroys the heavenly marriage of the will and the understanding in each individual mind.

Inmost Adultery

The inmost form of adultery is to reject the Lord and His Word altogether—*not even believing in them.* This is one step worse than theoretically believing in the Lord and yet being unfaithful to Him. Even if our belief is only theoretical, it can grow deeper, when we repent by amending our life. But if we deny the Divinity of the Lord Jesus Christ and consequently the holiness and authority of the Word (where His Divinity is proclaimed), there is no possibility of our repenting and being forgiven, for the simple reason that we do not *want* to be forgiven. This most grievous form of adultery involves turning away from the Lord to some other authority—usually our own self-derived intelligence, making this a god, putting it in the first place. Adultery in its inmost sense is really the same thing as idolatry—turning away to some other god than the Lord.

These three levels form a unit, so that the last and lowest contains the higher forms within it. There is a cause-and-effect relationship between the inmost form and the lower forms. Consequently, in the Christian world, whenever there is a general increase in turning away from the Lord Jesus Christ to some other authority, which is idolatry or the inmost form of adultery, there is a corresponding general increase in the outer and outmost forms of adultery. The three levels of adultery form a unit. Society as a *whole* experiences this tendency, though not every individual person who denies the Divinity of the Lord automatically becomes an adulterer.

The commandment forbidding adultery contains the very essence of religion itself. Yet this commandment is the one most frequently attacked, the commandment that some people would most like to do away with, because its purpose (the protection and preservation of a spiritual kind of marriage) has not been recognized.

Most people throughout history have seen the wisdom of having laws prohibiting murder, stealing, and false witness, because they can easily see these evils as potential dangers to their own person, their own possessions, and their reputation. But an increasing number of people today are being seduced by the idea that adultery is different, that it is simply a matter of one's own private life, having no consequences for the common good.

Adultery is a form of stealing. If stealing becomes rampant in society, it destroys all justice, all love and concern for the neighbor, and all mutual trust. This applies no less to stealing the affections of someone else's married partner. In addition to that, it undermines and destroys the institution of marriage and the home. And when these are destroyed, what is left in a society? Broken homes mean broken children, and broken children mean broken adults eventually coming into society. How can it be seriously maintained, then, that adultery is just a private matter, having nothing to do with the common good? The more cases of adultery there are and the more publicity given to them, the more the institution of marriage and the home is undermined, and the more society is torn asunder.

Stealing

There are also three layers of meaning within the commandment forbidding stealing. Stealing is taking what belongs to someone else or depriving people of the *use* of what really belongs to them, as in vandalism. Anyone who deliberately deprives a person of the use of some article might as well actually have stolen the article. Stealing extends much more widely than the clandestine theft of another's wealth or possessions, as in embezzlement or shop-lifting. It includes open robberies, plundering and looting; secret, hidden frauds that deprive people of their goods; all illicit gain, fraudulent expense accounts, fraudulent insurance claims, frauds in paying taxes and customs duties and in repaying debts; and cheating in examinations. Any false pretenses that cheat people out of their rights or goods and services are sins against this commandment. The following specific examples of stealthy and deceitful acquisition are listed in *True Christian Religion*: "Laborers who do their work unfaithfully and deceitfully; merchants, when they practice deceit in their merchandise, in weight, in measure, and in their accounts; . . . judges, when they give judgment for friendship, reward, relationship or other reasons, preventing law and evidence, and so depriving others of the goods which they rightfully possess" (*True Christian Religion* 317).

Vandalism is a form of stealing because it deprives people of the use of the article damaged. Cheating is stealing because it is the means of acquiring something to which one is not entitled, such as certain qualifications which open the way to higher positions of employment.

Spiritual Theft

Stealing in its literal meaning has to do with our life in *this world*. But there is a *spiritual* form of stealing as well. This refers not to the goods and riches of this world but to the "treasures in heaven" (Matthew 6:20) as well—*spiritual* riches, or the things learned from the Word of God about what is true and what is good. The Word of God is the treasure house of all these spiritual, eternal riches. Stealing away the spiritual wealth of the Word from anyone is spiritual theft; it robs a person of the *means* to spiritual life.

God's Word is stolen away from us by insinuating doubts about its holiness or when "the cares of this world and the deceitfulness of riches" (Matthew 13:22) lead to neglecting it. Those who try to persuade people that the Bible is not essentially different from any other ancient and historic book—that it is merely a human record of our developing idea of God—are spiritual thieves, stealing a person's spiritual riches.

We can also rob ourselves by allowing evils and the false ideas that confirm them to develop unchecked in our minds. These evils are the thieves that break in and steal, robbing us even of the information about spiritual things that we *seemed* to have had, but which has quietly disappeared from our memory. We certainly can do something about the loves and delights in ourselves that incline us to neglect the Word so that our ignorance of its teachings surpasses our knowledge of them. We can fight against and reject the feelings in us that incline us to agree with the theories of those who would rob us of the Word of God, the basis of spiritual or eternal life.

Inmost Theft

In the inmost sense, stealing is stealing from the *Lord*.

We steal from the Lord when we take credit for the good and truth that come forth from the Lord. If we take credit for any good feelings and true thoughts that we may have, we are stealing in the inmost sense; we are stealing from the Lord. The ascription at the end of the Lord's Prayer, "Yours is the kingdom, and the power, and the glory" (Matthew 6:13) becomes meaningless when we attribute these spiritual riches to ourselves, *misappropriating* them, stealing in the inmost sense.

An outstanding example of a spiritual thief in this inmost sense is given in the Lord's parable about the Pharisee praying in the Temple: "The Pharisee stood and prayed thus with himself, 'God, I thank You that I am not like other men—extortioners, unjust, adulterers, or even as this tax collector. I fast twice a week; I give tithes of all that I possess'" (Luke 18:11, 12). He is a spiritual thief, stealing the credit from the Lord, stealing the glory for himself.

Whoever shuns this inmost degree of theft as a sin against the Lord will also feel a revulsion against all the other forms of stealing that flow forth from it. If we really acknowledge that everything good and true comes from the Lord, and if we are therefore very careful not to steal the kingdom, the power and the glory from Him, we will be all the more likely to regard the Word of God with feelings of reverence and holiness. We will always be trying to protect the Word from falsification, so that it may serve its use as the indispensable means of attaining spiritual life. We will refrain from anything that will deprive our neighbor or ourselves of heavenly life. On the natural plane we will turn away in horror from every kind of illicit gain or craftiness. We shun all these evils because we have first of all shunned stealing from the Lord.

Both the spiritual murderer and the spiritual thief deprive us of our faith and charity. Yet there a difference. The murderer is violent. The murderer *attacks* our religious beliefs and openly ridicules them, so that in the end we feel *foolish* for attempting to maintain our beliefs. The spiritual *thief*, however, acts stealthily, so that we hardly realize that we have lost anything precious. In addition, he makes us feel *wise* for having accepted his opinions.

In *The Doctrine of Life* 81, Swedenborg makes this arresting statement: "The evil of theft enters more deeply into a person than any other evil, because it is conjoined with cunning and deceit." Subsequent passages go on to explain that cunning and deceit close the mind against any higher, heavenly influences. They close the mind against the Lord so that a person can never be made heavenly without a determined amendment of life, which is repentance.

False Witness

This reference to deceit leads us to discuss the next commandment: "You shall not bear false witness against your neighbor"(Exodus 20:16).

Have you ever stopped to think of how much evil is involved in bearing false witness against one's neighbor? Imagine standing up in court and falsely accusing an innocent person, *knowing* that he or she is innocent, making this deliberate declaration on oath in the name of the Lord! Blasphemy against the Lord and profanation are involved, as well as complete ruthlessness and cruelty, for the false witness has no compassion for the person unjustly suffering the punishment intended for someone else. The heartless destruction of the victim's good name, the loss of freedom and possibly of physical life, to say nothing of the complete disregard for justice and for the welfare of those dear to the one falsely accused, are all evils flowing from false witness.

Besides doing harm to the victim, those who swear a false oath do harm to themselves. They have shown their contempt for the truth—for reality. They have shown that they love themselves above all else, even more than the Lord, because the motive behind all such false witness is the protection of self or some reward to self. Self-love lies behind it in every case.

But false oaths and declarations before a judge are not the only forms of false witness or "the witness of a lie," as Swedenborg calls it. Any kind of lying—before anyone or to anyone, or even to oneself in one's own thoughts (as in self-justification)—is false witness. *Lying* means deliberately saying something *while knowing* it to be untrue. Saying things that are untrue when we fully and sincerely believe that they are, in fact, true is not lying; it is making a mistake, the result of a faulty understanding. No evil will is involved, no intention to deceive, no desire to cover up one's tracks, no desire to protect what is evil, as is always the case in deliberate lying.

But outright falsehoods are not the only way of bearing false witness. Sometimes lying is perpetrated by insinuations, by half-truths, by withholding some information, by quoting out of context, by exaggerating in favor of self, and by belittling the achievements of those whom we consider to be enemies. Other examples of bearing false witness include secret plots, cunning treachery, and defending wrong-doing to protect the interests of one's political party.

"A white lie," however, is different. "White lies" are not minor, slight departures from the truth. The "whiteness" of a lie depends upon the purity of the intention. For instance, when some little child shows us his unrealistic drawing of what he calls "a horse," we do not tell the brutal truth to the little child—that his drawing is nothing like a horse—because we do not wish to discourage him. We are fearful of perhaps depriving the world of a Rembrandt, so we tell a "white lie," a falsehood that springs from a good, laudable intention, with no selfishness or evil in it, but a love of one's neighbor. We are looking to *good*. Many similar situations in our lives arise from a desire to encourage people, so we say things that are not strictly in accordance with the truth—"*white* lies."

False witness also includes the *living* of a lie, hypocrisy or pretense. The quality of the act depends upon the intention involved. For example, pretending friendship for the sake of some ulterior motive such as self-advantage is "the witness of a lie."

It is also possible to bear false witness against others and so harm them even when we *intended no harm.* For example, we may make some rash accusation against a person whom we do not particularly like. The fact that she annoys us may cause us to jump to conclusions about her and impute the worst possible motives rather than entertain the possibility that she may be acting from a good motive. When we discover that we were mistaken, we may indeed feel very sorry for the harm we have done to her reputation and usefulness. Rash accusations can be "the witness of a lie." (For a classic example of a rash accusation and its consequences, see Joshua 22.)

That is why the law was given in Deuteronomy that all accusations were to be thoroughly investigated. If it turned out that someone had raised a false report against his neighbor, then the people were to do the harm to that false witness that had fallen upon his victim (see Deuteronomy 19:16–20).

A thorough investigation has to be made. We can only wish that the laws of evidence that every law student has to master should be part of *everyone's* education. A sincere desire to know what the truth really is, together with a commitment to the laws of evidence, would surely reduce the number of rash accusations against a neighbor or cases of relaying ill-founded rumors and gossip, or even self-justification—all of them the witness of a lie .

Spiritual Lying

With regard to spiritual life, *false witness* means "confirming falsity," the *defense of evil* that springs from a love of evil. When people so delight in committing evils that they *defend* them by arguments in order to make them appear as good, when they are convinced (and seek to persuade others) that evil things are good and that good is contemptible or laughable, they have reached the limit of their downward path. This is the clearest and most unashamed manifestation of evil. It is the end.

The understanding side of the mind is meant to be free from the influence of the evil feelings of our natural will, and capable of being raised above those evils in order to see *reality*. The understanding is meant to be able to see the truth—even if we do not like the truth or reality that we see. For example, if we can recognize an evil in ourselves—if we can see in our intellect or understanding that it is wrong and that we ought not to feel, think, act or speak from that evil—then our understanding is rising above our will. We are seeing things as they really are, seeing them in the light of heaven. Without that capability, we cannot be saved from evil.

If, however, our understanding is blinded—if we defend our evils by making up arguments to condone them and make them appear as good—then there is no hope of redemption. From that point onward we would be the witness of a lie, guilty of bearing false witness against the neighbor in a spiritual sense. Allowing the understanding to reason against what is good and confirm what is evil is false witness in the spiritual meaning of this commandment. "If your eye is bad, your whole body will be full of darkness. If therefore the light that is in you is darkness, how great is that darkness!" (Matthew 6:23).

The two sources of falsity are ignorance and evil. We have not been discussing the kind of falsity that arises from ignorance, but the falsity that springs from an evil heart, which always works against the neighbor spiritually understood, that is, against the Lord's kingdom wherever it appears.

Inmost Lying

In the inmost sense, as we might expect, *false witness* means to deny the existence of God, to blaspheme against Him and His Word. It is from this, the greatest and most far-reaching of the falsities of evil, that all the others come forth, even down to the last and lowest: the deliberate and calculated swearing of a false oath for the sake of self or the protection of self. The denial of the Lord—not from ignorance or from an imperfect understanding, but from an evil heart—has concealed within it every form of evil-speaking and false witness.

Even in the natural or literal sense, all forms of evil culminate in lying. The murderer, the adulterer, the thief, must all at some time utter a lie or *live* a lie in order to escape detection and punishment. False witness is always the defense mechanism of the evildoer.

Likewise, spiritual murderers, who from self-love obliterate the Lord from their thought and murder the spiritual lives of others by destroying the life of religion, in the end come to believe only what is false, what seems to condone their hatreds. Spiritual adulterers, who turn away from the Lord to some other god—that is, to the authority of their own ideas, and so adulterate the Divine truth of the Word, have already set out to be witnesses of a lie. Spiritual robbers, who steal from the Lord by taking to themselves the credit for a good love or a true thought, and who, as a consequence, come to deny the Word as the source of truth, are confirming the appearance instead of the reality. They are judging from the outward appearance, not the inner reality. They are already false witnesses. All degrees of evil, or all the manifestations of the loves of self and the world, end in falsity—the witness of a lie. "Brood of vipers! How can you, being evil, speak good things? For out of the abundance of the heart the mouth speaks. A good man out of the good treasure of his heart brings forth good things, and an evil man out of the evil treasure brings forth evil things" (Matthew 12:34–35).

In deliberate, premeditated false witness, all hell is present. False witness is the most complete and final manifestation and embodiment of the loves of hell: it is the unforgivable sin because people who indulge in false witness do not *wish* to be forgiven; they only wish to cover up.

(The chart on the next page summarizes what we have seen about these various levels of evil).

Why Were the Ten Commandments Divinely Revealed?

Every sensible person can see that murders, adulteries, thefts, and false witness must be forbidden because they destroy society. Any country that does not enforce laws forbidding these evils soon perishes in chaos. The law of reason also dictates that since these evils must not be done *in general* in a country, they should therefore not be done by any *individual* citizen in the country. A general thing is made up of particular things. An orchard is no better than the individual trees that make it to be an orchard.

In view of these considerations a question might arise as to why the Israelitish nation needed to have the Ten Commandments revealed *from heaven*. This question is addressed in the following passage from *True Christian Religion* 282:

> There is not a nation in the whole world which does not know that it is wicked to murder, to commit adultery, to steal, and to bear false witness, and that kingdoms, republics, and every form of organized society would be at an end unless these evils were guarded against by laws. Who then can suppose that the Israelitish nation was so stupid beyond all others as not to know that these things are evils? Anyone therefore may wonder that laws so universally known in the world should have been promulgated from Mount Sinai by Jehovah Himself in so miraculous a way. But listen: they were promulgated in so miraculous a way to make known that these laws are not only civil and moral laws, but also *Divine* laws; and that acting contrary to them is not only doing evil to the neighbor, that is, to a fellow-citizen and society, but is *also sinning against God.* For this reason these laws, by their promulgation by Jehovah from Mount Sinai, were made also *laws of religion.* Obviously, whatever Jehovah commands, He

	Murder	Adultery	Stealing	False Witness
3. *The Lord*	Hatred of the Lord Wishing to blot out His name	Denying Divinity of the Lord Turning to another authority	Stealing glory from the Lord Self-righteousness	Blaspheming the Lord and His Word
2. The Lord's Kingdom	Killing spiritual life of people Killing faith and charity	Adulterating goods of the Word Falsifying its truths (Mixing good and evil, truth and falsity)	Stealing another's faith and charity (by stealth)	Teaching evil as good and falsity as truth
1. Physical and Social	Hatred, Revenge Ostracism Injury Attempted murder Act of Murder	Lust, thinking anything lascivious and obscene Speaking obscenities Act of Adultery	Covetousness Misappropriation Fraud, ill-gotten gains Act of Theft or of Robbery	Self-deception Defamation Lying, Deceit Perjury

commands in order that it may be a matter of *religion*, and thus something to be done for the sake of salvation.

That teaching not only answers the question, but introduces the concept of motive. No action is any better than the motive from which it is done. The motive imparts the quality. Our obedience to the Ten Commandments takes on a *spiritual* quality when it is done for the reason that "God spoke all these words" (Exodus 20:1). We obey out of regard for the *Lord's* wishes.

Any atheist can see from the law of reason that these evils are harmful to society. But only a person with a religious motivation will shun them as *sins* against God.

Who Is the Real Victim?

The question of motive also introduces us into a deeper question: Who is the real victim?

The harmful effects of these evils on others and on society in general need no more emphasis. But what does need to be emphasized is the harm done to the *doer* of the evils. It is not only the *object* or victim of evil actions who suffers, but also the *subject* or doer. We have seen this already. We have seen that whoever is angry with his brother is in danger of the judgment (Matthew 5:22). Long before the evil feelings and attitudes belonging to the loves of self and the world come forth into open act and show themselves finally in the forms of murder, adultery, theft, and false witness; long before they do harm to someone outside the person who harbors these feelings, they have already done harm to that person. If people entertain feelings of hatred, they are victims of their hatred long before the object of their hatred. Haters are the real victims, because they have placed themselves under the influence of hell and are enveloped in its sphere. They are making their bed in hell. That is why it is said that evils should not be done "because they belong to the devil and are from the devil." "Whoever commits sin is a slave of sin" (John 8:34). Frequently, the harm done to another is limited to the victim's natural, *terminal* life. But the harm done to the subject or doer of evil always relates to one's *spiritual* life, life to eternity. As the Lord said: "Do not fear those who kill the body but cannot kill the soul. But rather fear Him who is able to destroy both soul and body in hell" (Matthew 10:28).

10

ESCAPING FROM
EVIL FEELINGS

It is an eternal truth . . . that everything of life flows in the good of life from the Lord, and the evil of life from hell.

Emanuel Swedenborg
Arcana Coelestia 6325

Evils are not to be done "because they belong to the devil and are from the devil." But what does the devil mean?

The Devil

The devil means hell "in the whole complex" (*The Apocalypse Explained* 1014:3). Abstractly, the devil means the evil that makes hell and flows forth from it, such as the loves of self and the world, the two devilish loves that rule in hell. The love of dominating from the love of self is also described as "the devil."

There is no basis in Scripture for the idea that the devil is a fallen angel.[1] The Lord pointed out in Luke 16 that there is a great gulf fixed between heaven and hell, so that those who wish to pass from heaven to hell cannot, nor can those come into heaven who would like to come out of hell (Luke 16:26). That verse presents a universal law admitting of no exceptions. The idea that Satan is only one person also needs to be reexamined.

Individual devils or demons or satans are certainly people; they had all lived hellish lives on earth. There is some truth, too, in the idea that the devil is *like* one person, just as the whole of heaven in one complex is like one person, whom Swedenborg calls the Greatest Man.

The church on earth as the "body of Christ" (Colossians 1:24; Ephesians 1:22, 23; 4:12) is a familiar idea. Any group or society of people in this world is like one person. All the functions performed in the human body are to be found in any group or community of people. In any town, city, or country, there are those who perform the function of the head: the *brainy* people. There are those who perform the function of the heart: the *hearty* people. There are those who perform the function of the hands: the *handy* people. And there are those (the vast majority) who do the "leg work," who perform the function of the legs and feet, the support of the whole body. All the functions of the various organs and members of the human body are performed by the people in any body or community of people. In agreement with this idea, the United States of America is sometimes represented as one man, named Uncle Sam, and Great Britain is referred to as John Bull.

It is a similar case with the church. The church is a "Greater Man." But heaven is the "Greatest Man." All the functions of the human body are performed by those who are now in the Lord's kingdom in the heavens. Viewed in this light, heaven in the aggregate could be said to be a "Grand Man."

---

[1] Biblical support for this statement is given in the appendix.

The societies of hell also are organized according to the functions of the human body. However, all those functions are performed unwillingly and under pressure by the inhabitants of hell, while in heaven they are performed willingly, in freedom. Hell is the opposite of the Greatest Man. "Hell is like a monstrous man" (*The Divine Providence* 302). "The universal hell represents one monstrous devil" (*True Christian Religion* 32:6). In this sense—and in this sense only—it could be said that the devil (or hell) is like a person.

Since *the devil* means "hell," our statement could be rephrased as: "Evils are not to be done because they belong to hell and are from hell."

Really seeing for ourselves that evils belong to hell and come from hell is vitally important. This insight is the first step in escaping from the burden of evil feelings, which can lead to evil actions. If we stop ourselves from contemplating or doing evils for any other reason, we are not really regarding them as sins against the Lord; we are not really fleeing from them in horror. We are only *suppressing* them, preventing them from appearing outwardly before the world. We really need to see that evil feelings flow in from hell.

This is indeed known in the Christian world, but for most people it is not really believed from the heart in any practical sense, in such a way as to affect one's life. We hear echoes of this idea when somebody describing a completely uncharacteristic action by an acquaintance, says, "I don't know what *got into* him," or "I don't know what *possessed* her." But people who use that form of language would probably be quite startled by our taking their words at face value, as if they really believed that evil feelings can flow in from evil spirits in hell and influence a person's behavior.

And yet this teaching is one of the most dynamic and practical in all of the deeper view of Christianity. When we really see that all life flows into us—good feelings from the Lord through heaven and evil feelings from hell—we have made a great step forward in our spiritual growth. Few things hold back would-be disciples of the

Lord more than the feeling that the good that they do is from themselves and the evil that they do originates in themselves. Claiming
the good for oneself leads to self-righteousness and a sense of merit;
claiming possession of hell's evil promptings can lead to evil actions
or to a paralyzing form of guilt and anxiety.

When we think according to the reality, we learn not to
identify ourselves with the evil feelings and desires that surge up
within us. We do not have to act as if we were the owners of these
feelings. We do not have to *identify* ourselves with them, saying:
"That's *me!* That's the way I am." We can just as easily say: "These
feelings are rising up from hell and flowing into my mind. I do not
have to accept them." We disown them, detach ourselves from them,
distance ourselves from them, realizing that they are separate from
us and should be *kept* separate from us. In this way, we are delivered
from them, set free. If only we would always act in accordance with
the reality, with the way things *really* are, we could be delivered from
all the evil feelings that flow in from hell and bind us to hell.

Unfortunately, however, it is very difficult for us in our natural, unregenerate state to believe that this is in fact the reality. We
are not aware, by any conscious sensation, of the presence of either
the angelic people who are in heaven or the devilish people who
have chosen hell as their abode. Because we do not feel their presence, and neither see nor hear them (in the vast majority of cases),
we do not know *from experience* that good feelings flow in from
heaven and evil feelings flow in from hell. We human beings need to
be told this by the Lord in His Divine Word. Otherwise, we would
never know. We need to learn this from a source outside of ourselves. For this reason, we must act according to what the Lord reveals; we have to eat of "the tree of life" rather than be guided by
ideas formed from our own sensations, which is to "eat of the tree of
the knowledge of good and evil" (Genesis 2:17). As Swedenborg explains in *Arcana Coelestia* 6206:

> The reason that evil is fastened onto man is that he believes and
> persuades himself that what he thinks and does is from himself,

and in this way makes it his own. If he believed as is really the case, then evil would not be appropriated to him; for the moment that evil flowed in, he would reflect that it was from the evil spirits with him, and as soon as he thought this, the angels would turn it aside and reject it. For the inflow from the angels is into what a man knows and believes, and not into what he does not know and does not believe; for that inflow is not fixed anywhere except where there is something belonging to the man.

The effect of applying that teaching varies from person to person. Most people speak of a great load or tension being lifted from their shoulders. But for one man, the effect was quite dramatic.

This man had come to me for help with his fierce temper. He felt that his wife was always cutting him down, which enraged him. "I've always had a bad temper," he explained, "but now I'm afraid it will get out of control." After discussing this with him for a little while, I quoted that teaching in *Arcana Coelestia* 6206 about how to be freed from the influx from hell. This gave him hope, but he wondered how he could remember that passage, as he had no copy of the *Arcana Coelestia*. I duplicated the relevant passage, which he put in his wallet.

A week later, when I asked if he had noticed any improvement, he exclaimed excitedly, "Oh yes, yes!" Taking the duplicated passage from his wallet and waving it around, he said, beaming: "This is magic! Whenever I feel an attack of rage coming on, I just pull this out and read it. It always works. It always calms me down!"

This association between the two worlds is an unconscious one. The inhabitants of hell, like the inhabitants of heaven, are quite unaware of the person with whom they are associated. They are no more conscious of him than he is aware of their presence with him. But they are *subconsciously* attracted by a person's feelings of delight that are in agreement with their own, an attraction of similar feelings. Thus, Swedenborg states in *Arcana Coelestia* 5851 that "If he is avaricious, there are spirits who are avaricious; if he is haughty, there are haughty spirits; if he is desirous of revenge, there are spirits of this character; if he is deceitful, there are similar spirits. Man summons to himself spirits from hell in accordance with his life."

So if we had no tendency to evil and if we had never contemplated doing an evil act, then we would receive no such inflow from the hells. There would be neither basis nor welcome for it. But there is always something in us that attracts and summons the presence of hell.

We need to acknowledge and confess this, especially when examining ourselves, being careful not to become overwhelmed by the knowledge that part of us welcomes hell. Because we have evil spirits as well as good ones for our spiritual companions, we are not therefore irretrievably evil and beyond redemption. We are perfectly free to separate ourselves from those inhabitants of hell who want to stir up the worst in us and induce us to act and speak from those evil feelings that flow forth from them. We can free ourselves from this inflow from hell by recollecting that all evils "belong to hell and are from hell."

But we have to do this promptly, in the very moment that we recognize evil flowing in. Fortunately, "evil that enters into the thought does no harm to the person, because evil is continually infused by spirits from hell, and is continually repelled by angels. But when evil enters into the will, then it does do harm, for then it also goes forth into act whenever external bonds do not restrain. Evil enters into the will by being kept in the thought, by consent, especially by act and the consequent delight," we are told in *Arcana Coelestia* 6204.

That is why we must act promptly. Otherwise, if we keep thinking about the feelings and consent to them, we will begin to enjoy them, the first step toward becoming "hooked."

A Powerful Thought

How can there be such power in the mere thought that what is evil has flowed in from hell? But is it really a mere thought? Is it *thought* alone or *truth* alone?

This thought is not an empty formula or technique; rather, it involves a complete attitude to life, a spiritual attitude, a way of thinking, feeling, believing, speaking, and acting, possible only to those who at heart acknowledge these two important truths:

1. That the Lord Jesus Christ is now Divine in both Soul and Body

2. That evils are sins (see *The Divine Providence* 321:5–6)

Acknowledging these two truths is not an arbitrary requirement. The reasons given are: that "those who do not acknowledge the Lord's Divinity, being disjoined from Him, believe that they think from themselves" and "those who do not acknowledge evils as sins . . . think from hell; and in hell everyone imagines that he thinks from himself" (*The Divine Providence* 321:6).

Without a heartfelt belief in these two truths, this "technique" simply will not work. A certain humility is required, flowing from the admission that a person is nothing in and from himself or herself without the Lord, and that the Lord is *everything*. This state of deep humility is essential for genuine worship of the Lord. Only from the goodness of such humility before the Lord can anyone have any power at all against the hells when reflecting that evil suggestions and thoughts are aroused by the inflow from hell. After all, it takes real humility before anyone will believe and use this truth.

A further reason for the power of this thought is that evil spirits cannot endure being reflected upon. Their strength is in their *secret* operation; they like darkness rather than light. Like criminals in this world, they abhor having the spotlight focused on their activities. Swedenborg gives many accounts, from experience, of spirits becoming indignant and departing when their true nature is exposed and proclaimed. They simply cannot withstand the atmosphere of heaven, which we summon whenever we think according to the reality.

The teaching that "evils should not be done because they belong to hell and are from hell" surely provides us with the strongest reason for turning our backs on evil feelings—in fact, fleeing away from them as we would flee away from some disgusting odor. But that teaching also shows us the way to free ourselves from evil feelings, by remembering that they do in fact belong to hell and not to us.

Social Implications

Tremendous social implications also flow from the principle we have been discussing. Can we not see that here we have the remedy for all the world's ills?

We can indeed, to some extent, control criminal acts (or acts against society) by external force, such as by public disapproval and law enforcement by police forces, armies, and courts of law. But we can never *eradicate* evil in that way. We can only limit and contain the *expression* of it, reducing its evil effects on our natural life.

To make a real onslaught on evil, however, we need to root out the cause of evil actions. Each one of us needs to begin with himself or herself, and refrain from doing evils for the sole reason that "they belong to hell and are from hell," or (what is the same) that they are sins against the Lord. The French philosopher Montaigne put it most aptly: "If you would reform the world, begin with yourself. Then there will be one rogue less in the world."

If every person in the world were to refrain from lusting after the evil feelings hidden within the criminal acts forbidden in the Ten Commandments for the reason that they "belong to hell and are from hell" (and thus are against the Lord), then no evil acts would be done outwardly. All the murders and crimes of violence;

all adulteries and attacks upon the institution of marriage; all cheating, fraud, and stealing; all deceit, lying, false witness, and defamation would disappear from the face of the earth. How infinitely good and wise is the Lord's advice, "First cleanse the inside of the cup and dish, that the outside of them may be clean also" (Matthew 23:26). This state of affairs, when not only external acts of evil but also the evil feelings that beget them no longer exist, is the complete "kingdom of God" or rule of God that we wish will come when we pray: "*Your* kingdom come. *Your* will be done on earth as it is in heaven" (Matthew 6:10).

Here we see the true mission of a church. Its aim, the ideal toward which it strives, is to encourage every one of its members to seek first the kingdom of God and His righteousness, to seek this in themselves by shunning their secret evils (and the falsities that seek to justify them) because they are sins against the Lord; and to encourage others outside of the church to live that same kind of life, the life of religion. This is the ideal, and we must ever keep it before our gaze.

However, we do have to realize that complete and absolute success will never be possible. Human freedom of choice cannot be ignored. The Lord allows each one of us to choose whether we will follow Him or not, and to what extent we are willing to give up self-gratification in order to follow Him. He grants this privilege of free choice to every human being, and He never takes it away.

Consequently, there will always be those who choose to follow the Lord only a little, and also those who reject Him and do not follow Him at all—in fact, who oppose Him and what comes from Him. Therefore, absolute success will never be achieved.

Nevertheless, we need to act *as if* the ideal were completely attainable. We need to keep striving toward the ideal. If we aim at anything less than the ideal, we will be satisfied with that lesser goal. That will then become our ideal, and our sights will be progressively lowered.

The Negative and the Positive Focus

The teaching that "to shun evils as sins is the Christian religion itself" (*The Divine Providence* 239) or, what is the same thing, that "evils should not be done because they belong to hell and are from hell," is sometimes thought to place too much emphasis on evil, focusing our attention too much on it. This, it is feared, could lead to a miserable, mournful state: the opposite of the happiness of heaven. If this were true, it would indeed be a very serious indictment.

But is it true? If we turn away from evils because they are from hell, we are doing so because to *some* extent, at least, we are concerned for the Lord; we realize that what is from hell is against the Lord and His kingdom. We have some love for the Lord. If we shun our evils because they are sins against the Lord, we are looking to the Lord and inviting His presence. And if we are looking to the Lord and are concerned for Him, are we not looking toward everything that is good and positive? Are we not looking toward goodness itself, the source of everything good? In fact, is it possible to be any more positive than that? It is really out of regard for the Lord that we shun our evils as *sins*.

That is why the full statement of the case in *The Doctrine of Charity* reads: "The first thing of charity is to look to the Lord and shun evils as sins; and the second thing of charity is to do good things" (*The Doctrine of Charity* 40). Besides this, the proportion in which people shun evils because they are sins is the proportion in which they do good things, not from themselves, but from the Lord. The proportion in which people shun murders of every kind as sins is the proportion in which they have love toward the neighbor. Similarly, to shun adultery as a sin is to love marriage undefiled by lasciviousness; to shun thefts of every kind as sins is to love sincerity; to shun false witness of every kind as sin is to love truthfulness. In other words, shunning evil as sin is always looking to doing what is good. (See *The Doctrine of Life* 18–31, 67–91.)

The idea that we should *first* shun evil before we can do what is good has always been basic to religion. In the Jewish Church, the Divine teaching was "Cease to do evil, learn to do good" (Isaiah 1:16–17). In the Christian Church it was "Repent, for the kingdom of heaven is at hand!" (Matthew 3:2)

Besides being the consistent teaching of Divine revelation throughout the ages, this teaching is confirmed by experience and common sense, as in this passage from *True Christian Religion* 511:

> Who can introduce sheep and kids and lambs into fields or woods where there are all kinds of wild beasts, before he has driven out the beasts? Who can make a garden out of a piece of ground that is overgrown with thorns, briars, and nettles, before he has rooted out those noxious weeds? Who can establish a mode of administering justice according to judicial practices in a city held by hostile forces and establish citizenship, before he has expelled those forces? It is the same with evils in man. They are like wild beasts, like thorns and briars, and like hostile forces; and the church can no more have a common abode with evils than a man can dwell in a cage where there are tigers and leopards.

Until we drive out the wild beasts in ourselves, eradicate the thorns and briars, and conquer the hostile forces, we will continue to be delighted by the evils forbidden in the Ten Commandments. By natural inclination, our human nature—twisted by hereditary tendencies and left entirely to itself and free to do what it likes—loves all forms of idolatry, blasphemy, irreverence, mockery, contempt, theft, adultery, murder, false witness, and covetousness. We can observe from experience that where society does not impose restraints, either by law or by moral sanctions, or where there is no real influence of the Word of God in a society, all the previously mentioned evils will break forth into open act.

Still, there is hope. We need not be imprisoned by our natural tendencies; we can rise above them, as we are assured in *True Christian Religion* 574:

Viewed in himself the natural man in no way differs in his nature from the nature of beasts. Like them he is wild; but it is as to his will that he is like that; in understanding he does differ from beasts, in that the understanding can be elevated above the lusts of the will, and not only see but also moderate them; and for this reason man is able to think from understanding, and speak from thought, which beasts cannot do.

So any good actions we do before evil motives are shunned as sins are not really good. They only *appear* to be good. Can a bad tree bring forth good fruit? (see Matthew 7:17–18) It is the motive that imparts the quality to an action. Actions done from evil motives may indeed be of use and benefit to the person to whom they are done. For example, if a group of poor people were helped very generously by a man because he was seeking some exalted office or some other honor for himself, then the poor people, as recipients of the good action, would say that they had benefitted. The man's actions had a good effect. But it would be of no benefit to the doer—the man himself. He could not claim that he had done what was good, because his good actions proceeded from a selfish and worldly motive. He was not interested in the welfare of others. It was only good from and for self, good from the man, which is not good at all. "The essence of good can be from no other source than Him who is good itself" (*The Doctrine of Life* 13). In order to do what is good, we need first to be working in conjunction with the Lord—the only source of what is good—and to be working in conjunction with the Lord, we have to begin by shunning our evils "because they belong to hell and are from hell."

This teaching was clearly stated in the New Testament in particular. In John we read that "a man can receive nothing unless it has been given to him from heaven" (John 3:27); and "he who abides in Me, and I in him, bears much fruit; for without Me you can do nothing" (John 15:5). Our human nature is so contrary to heaven that it must be exchanged for a new nature. Human nature cannot be *changed,* only *exchanged.* "Unless one is born again, he cannot see the kingdom of God" (John 3:3).

Evil feelings or desires flow in from hell. In turning our backs upon the hellish inflow because it is against the Lord, we are actually looking to Him and loving Him. The extent to which we are conjoined with Him, the one source of goodness, is the extent to which we are doing good that is really good.

WHEN GOOD DEEDS ARE REALLY GOOD

Good things should be done because they belong to God and are from God.

Emanuel Swedenborg
True Christian Religion 3:2

Goods or good deeds are the same as "uses" (as Swedenborg calls them). They are good deeds done from the Lord, not from self: actions that benefit others and the common good.

What a world it would be if doing these good deeds or "uses" were the norm rather than the exception! The Lord's kingdom would have come; His will would be done on earth as it is in heaven. At last, we would literally have heaven on earth.

Heaven is a kingdom of uses, a kingdom where the inhabitants derive their highest and most abiding happiness from performing uses or good services to others, both in general and with each individual person.

The very best of these good actions are of lasting, eternal benefit; they are not just a matter of temporary relief. Since a church is meant to be an image of heaven or a receptacle of heavenly loves, it is meant to be the means of conjoining heaven and earth. Consequently, "the best [works] are those that are done for the sake of the uses of the church," as we are informed in *The Apocalypse Explained* 975:2.

The Lord always looks to eternal ends or purposes—to the eternal welfare of everyone—in everything that He does from His Divine love by means of His Divine wisdom. He uses temporal things—the things of this ephemeral world and life—only as a means to eternal ends. Whenever we do good things that "belong to God and are from God," we are becoming an image and likeness of Him. We are looking, perhaps unconsciously, to the eternal welfare of everyone with whom we have any dealings, using temporal, worldly things as means to eternal ends.

Suppose we learn that a friend or acquaintance is contemplating receiving a sizable sum of money from an insurance company by withholding some relevant information that would make him or her ineligible to benefit. There seems to be no risk of being found out. In that situation, we can either aid and abet the crime by keeping quiet, or we can seek to raise the person's thought to a higher, more eternal level. Lecturing that person or expressing shock or indignation would be worse than useless, even counterproductive. But, like Socrates, we could ask some awkward questions: "Have you considered the total situation? Have you considered the implications of what you are planning to do? Have you asked yourself what God would have you do in this situation? Have you prayed about this?"

The other person may well become angry and abusive, seeing us as a "spoil-sport," especially if he or she has no spiritual conscience or one that is sleeping. But we have planted a thought that offers a different course of action. We have brought God into the equation. Who knows what effect that thought may have after the person has left our presence and quietly thinks it over? Even a dormant conscience can be aroused.

Looking to the eternal welfare of others is an example of loving others as the Lord loves us. "A new commandment I give to you, that you love one another; as I have loved you, that you also love one another" (John 13:34).

The word for *to love* used in that passage means, in the original, "to consider the welfare of," which is the essential meaning of the much abused word *love*. Another word for love is also used in the New Testament, but never when we are *commanded* to love. The meaning of that other word is simply "to be fond of." To be fond of another cannot be commanded, but God may certainly command us to consider the welfare of others, just as He considers our welfare—our eternal welfare.

We can do these good things only from God. "With men this is impossible, but with God all things are possible" (Matthew 19:26). "Without Me you can do nothing" (John 15:5). Any attempt to do good things from our own powers will be contaminated by selfishness and thoughts of worldly status.

The following passages from Swedenborg's works have the same central theme, but each one presents some additional facet of the truth:

> Charity is willing well, and good works are doing well from willing well. Charity and works are distinct from each other like will and action, or like the mind's affection and the body's operation; consequently like the internal man and the external; and these two are related to each other like cause and effect, since the causes of all things are formed in the internal man, and from this are all effects produced in the external. Therefore charity, since it belongs to the internal man, is willing well; and works, since they belong to the external man, are doing well from willing well." (*True Christian Religion* 374)

Heaven and Hell 358 even says that "acting is willing, and speaking is thinking," so that where the Word of God says that we will be judged and rewarded according to our deeds, the meaning is that we will be judged and rewarded according to our thoughts and affections, the *source* of our deeds. "Otherwise [any action] would be nothing but a movement like that of an automaton" (*Heaven and Hell* 472). The same passage concludes by pointing out that "a thousand people may ... do similar deeds, so alike in outward form as to be almost undistinguishable, and yet each one regarded in itself be different, because from an unlike will" (see also The *Doctrine of Charity* 4 and 8).

Who Is My Neighbor?

These good works are to be done to one's neighbor. But who is one's neighbor?

That question was put to the Lord by a student of the law of Moses, a man who wished to test the Lord's fidelity to that law (Luke 10:25–29). He knew from the Scriptures that he must love his neighbor, but he wished to know how the Lord understood the term *one's neighbor*. The usual interpretation at that time was that only a person of one's own nation was a neighbor to be loved, that is, helped.

The Lord answered his question with the well-known parable of the Good Samaritan:

> Then Jesus answered and said, "A certain man went down from Jerusalem to Jericho, and fell among thieves, who stripped him of his clothing, wounded him, and departed, leaving him half dead. Now by chance a certain priest came down that road. And when he saw him, he passed by on the other side. Likewise a Levite, when he arrived at the place, came and looked, and passed by on the other side. But a certain Samaritan, as he journeyed, came where he was. And when he saw him, he had compassion. So he went to him, and bandaged his wounds, pouring on oil and wine; and he set him on his own animal, brought him to an inn, and took care of him. On the next day, when he departed, he took out

two denarii, gave them to the innkeeper, and said to him, 'Take care of him; and whatever more you spend, when I come again, I will repay you.' So which of these three do you think was neighbor to him who fell among the thieves?" And he said, "He who showed mercy on him." Then Jesus said to him, "Go and do likewise." (Luke 10:30–37)

The question was, "Who is my neighbor?" The answer was, "He who showed mercy on him." The good Samaritan, the one who did what is good, is the neighbor to be loved, helped, and encouraged.

The original hearers of that parable must have been greatly shocked by a Samaritan's being made the hero. In fact, at that time the Samaritans were despised, although geographically they were "neighbors." So the Lord's purpose in making the hero of the story a citizen of Samaria was to broaden the prevailing idea of "one's neighbor," expanding it beyond the boundaries of one's own country.

A person who is doing any good thing is one's neighbor no matter of what nationality or race. Strictly speaking, our neighbor is not a person at all, but the good feelings or good attitudes that person has received from the Lord. Because all goodness is from the Lord, He is the neighbor in the highest sense. The Lord is inmostly the Good Samaritan.

Because goodness is the neighbor that is to be loved, fostered, and helped, the Theological Writings of Emanuel Swedenborg always refer to *the* neighbor, not *one's* neighbor. Anyone is the neighbor to be loved and helped according to the quantity and quality of the goodness that person has received from the Lord.

So, one who obeys only the *letter* of the law is not so much the neighbor as one who acts from the *spirit* of the legal code or from *moral* goodness. People are the neighbor to an even greater extent if they act from *spiritual* goodness or obedience to the Divine commandments. Since one who acts from spiritual goodness will be both a moral person and a law-abiding citizen, we are to seek first spiritual goodness, then the lesser goods (moral and civic) will be added. "Seek first the kingdom of God and His righteousness, and all these things shall be added to you" (Matthew 6:33).

Yet feelings of charity by themselves do not produce genuinely good works any more than the will alone can do anything. We can wish and wish to do something good and helpful until our heart is at a bursting point, but that accomplishes nothing. We need to know *how* to do it; we need some enlightenment from our intellect or understanding. Otherwise, we will be like the sadly misguided woman who thought she could dry out her drenched pet dog by putting him in the microwave! Or like the man who, passing his vacationing friend's house and noticing that the lights were on, switched them off at the main switch, not realizing that his friend's refrigerator was stacked with fish! The consequences of these acts of misguided charity are unbearable to contemplate, and examples are plentiful. In such cases the heart (the will) is in the right place, but the head (the understanding) leaves much to be desired.

It is similar with regard to our spiritual life: charity in the will needs to be matched with an enlightened faith (the sight of truth) in the understanding.

For example, aiding and abetting a murderous escaped convict "out of the kindness of our heart" is charity alone, merely natural sentimental charity. Such misguided charity ignores the larger picture, the welfare and protection of society as a whole. Charity alone is in the dark, lacking the wisdom provided by the truth belonging to an enlightened faith, which by its very nature causes us to look to the Lord and His eternal purposes. A spiritual kind of faith allows us to view life in the perspective of eternity.

Another example of charity enlightened by faith would be the technique, often used in child raising, known as "tough love."

Charity and Faith Together

The need for charity and faith to work together is brought out in this passage from *True Christian Religion* 377:

> Good works are not produced by charity alone, still less by faith alone, but by charity and faith together. This is because charity apart from faith is not charity, and faith apart from charity is not faith. Because of this, charity cannot exist by itself or faith by itself; and it cannot be said that charity in itself produces any good works, or faith in itself. . . . Consequently, when a person does good works in accordance with truths, he does them in light, that is, intelligently and wisely. The conjunction of charity and faith is like the marriage of husband and wife. From the husband as a father and the wife as a mother all natural offspring are born; and in like manner from charity as a father and faith as a mother all spiritual offspring, which are things known about good and truth, are born. . . . Neither the husband alone nor the wife alone can produce offspring.

The good actions that are to be done "because they belong to God and are from God" have to go forth from the goodness of charity conjoined with the truth that belongs to faith—both from the Lord.

Levels of the Neighbor

Swedenborg deepens our idea of the neighbor to be loved by showing that the goodness received from the Lord is the neighbor; he also widens our view, extending the neighbor beyond the good received by one individual to include the goodness in

- a group of individuals
- one's country
- the whole human race
- the church

- the Lord's kingdom, including the heavens
- supremely, the Lord Himself

These are ascending levels or degrees of the neighbor, like rungs on a ladder, as in Jacob's vision of a ladder (Genesis 28: 10–13). At the top of the ladder was the Lord, the source and origin of the neighbor. Wherever good is received, *there* is the neighbor to whom or to which good things are to be done—from God. In a word, charity toward the neighbor means fostering and enhancing the reception of goodness from the Lord, wherever it is received.

Since these levels of the neighbor are like rungs on a ladder, the higher ones are to be preferred to the lower ones. Therefore, a group of individuals is more the neighbor than one individual; one's country is more the neighbor than a group within the country; the whole human race is the neighbor in a still higher degree than one's country; the church is the neighbor in a still higher degree, because it is concerned with the *eternal* life of others; the Lord's kingdom is an even higher level of the neighbor because it consists of all who are in a state of goodness, whether on earth or in heaven. The Lord, being the source of the goodness that is the neighbor on all these levels, is supremely the neighbor to be loved (see *The New Jerusalem and Its Heavenly Doctrine* 91–96).

The ascending levels of the neighbor are a great guide in decision making, imparting much-needed clarity. For example, a church organization that is essentially a social club focusing mainly on worldly goals is less the neighbor to be loved and helped than one in which the Lord's kingdom is the main focus. Similarly, a country fostering the eternal welfare of its citizens by means of churches and freedom of religion is more the neighbor than one where churches are banned.

Day-to-Day Charity

Charity is meant to be the motivating force in every area of our daily life, and it is much more widespread than "caring for widows and orphans, contributing to the building of hospitals, infirmaries, asylums, orphans' homes, and especially of churches, and to their decorations and income" (*True Christian Religion* 425). Charity certainly includes these things, and we must do them, but doing good is not limited to those activities.

Being charitable enters into our occupation, our worship, our good works, our obligations or duties, and even into our recreation.

Charity in Our Occupation

The genuinely good works of charity begin with our occupation or employment. Here, especially, we must do "good things because they belong to God and are from God." People who are looking to the Lord and shunning their evils as sins, and who are consequently carrying out the duties of their employment sincerely, honestly, and faithfully, are doing good from the Lord all day long (see The *Doctrine of Charity* 158–182). Doing good things is not a part-time occupation that begins only *after* work. Charity begins *with* our work. Our occupation gives us untold opportunities for doing good things, performing uses and services to others. In fact, this is the primary and most important means of expressing love for the neighbor.

> Charity may be defined as doing good to the neighbor daily and continually, not only to the neighbor individually, but also to the neighbor collectively; and this can be done only through doing what is good and just in the office, business, and employment in which a person is engaged, and with those with whom he has any dealings; for this is one's daily work, and when he is not doing it, it still occupies his mind continually, and he has it in thought and intention. (*True Christian Religion* 423)

Since we need to know how good works or uses are to be done in various occupations, this knowledge has been provided. In Swedenborg's short work on charity, several specific examples are given of the way good works or uses are to be done in the following occupations: a priest, a magistrate, and the officials under a magistrate, a judge, the commander of an army and the officers under a commander, a common soldier, a merchant or businessperson, a worker, a farmer, a ship's captain and sailors, and finally servants (The *Doctrine of Charity* 158–172). There is, obviously, no lack of teaching on how charity applies in our occupation.

At least half our waking hours during the working week are taken up with the duties of our work, which makes our occupations the most constant and widespread instrument for being of use to others and to the common good.

Charity in Worship

Good things may also pervade our worship. Feelings of charity or goodwill flow in from the Lord to the extent that we shun our evils as sins. Then "all the acts of worship that are performed externally are signs [or manifestations] of" charity (*The Doctrine of Charity* 177). When we receive these good feelings, our worship is "from the heart," not just from the lips and the lungs, a sign or indication of charity within and a good thing done from the Lord.

Charity in Good Works

Good works are commonly called benefactions, good kind deeds that we are moved to do voluntarily. "But most of these things are not properly matters of charity, but extraneous to it" (*True Christian Religion* 425), for "charity and works are distinct from each other like will and action" (*True Christian Religion* 374). In fact, "no one is saved through these benefactions, but through the charity from which they are done, and which is therefore in those benefactions.

These benefactions are outside of the person, but charity is within him; and everyone is saved according to the quality of the good or charity in him" (*The Doctrine of Charity* 185).

Nevertheless, these benefactions *should* be done, but prudently and from charity (*True Christian Religion* 425–428). They are done prudently when we consider the kind of life the recipient is leading. If we do not do this, we may well be doing good to evildoers, and so encouraging evil itself. For example, if we give a murderer a gun, we are not being charitable. We may also unwittingly confirm lazy people in their laziness or irresponsible people in their irresponsibility. After all, good from the Lord is what is to be loved and fostered.

Charity in Duties

We all have certain obligations or duties beyond the duties of our occupation. Some of them are public, relating to the requirements of government—local, state, and national—for example, paying taxes (*True Christian Religion* 430) and customs duties (*The Doctrine of Charity* 187). These duties are done from goodwill by people moved by spiritual charity, who from the Lord look to their country's welfare and "regard it as iniquitous to deceive or defraud" (*True Christian Religion* 430). Obligations of employers to their employees, and of employees to employers are public duties. What a different world it would be if most people had a spiritual conscience with regard to their public duties!

In the home we have domestic duties: those of a husband toward his wife and of a wife toward her husband, those of fathers and mothers toward their children and of children toward their parents. These duties also can be done unwillingly from self or cheerfully from the Lord—from the good feelings of charity or goodwill that come from the Lord.

We also incur duties of a private nature, such as paying wages and bills, paying interest, fulfilling contracts, guarding securities, and some matters that become obligations because of a solemn promise. Keeping promises is meant to be a private duty of charity.

Charity in Recreation

Even our recreational activities—called by Swedenborg "the diversions of charity"—are included in the good things to be done from the Lord. These diversions or recreations are "various delights and pleasures of the bodily senses, useful for the recreation of the mind" (*The Doctrine of Charity* 189). We all know from experience that if our mind is not relaxed—if kept at the stretch all the time—its affections become dull, like salt that has lost its savor or "like a bended bow, which, unless it is unbent, loses the power that it derives from its elasticity. Just so the mind if kept from day to day in the same ideas, without variety" (*The Doctrine of Charity* 190).

For those who are employed, these diversions (or "turnings aside") are "diversions of employments." They are really diversions of the *affections* from which we do our work. As those affections are various in quality, so are our recreations. "They are one thing if the affection of charity is in them, another if there is in them an affection for honor only, another if there is an affection only for gain, another if they perform their duties only for the sake of support and the necessaries of life, another if only for a name so that they may be famous, or if only for the sake of salary so that they may grow rich, or that they may live in style, and so on" (*The Doctrine of Charity* 192).

What if charity from the Lord is present in these diversions or recreations? In that case the delight of being useful continues deep within them and is gradually renewed. "A longing for one's work breaks or ends them. For the Lord flows into them from heaven and renews; and He also gives an interior sense of pleasure in them, which those who are not in the affection of charity know nothing of. He breathes into them a fragrance, or, as it were, a sweetness perceptible only to oneself" (*The Doctrine of Charity* 193).

So those delights are entirely unknown to people who are not doing good from the Lord. Such heavenly delights seem incredible to them, because people like that have never experienced those deeper delights, and cannot understand anyone's having a longing to return to his or her work. Those who perform the duties of their calling from necessity and from selfish motives remote from service to others live for the weekend and recreation. "[T]heir duties are burdens to them" (*The Doctrine of Charity* 196).

All these examples show how good from the Lord is meant to penetrate every single activity of our lives. No area is exempt; everything is changed. "Behold! I make all things new" (Revelation 21:5).

A Call to Action

These good things need to be actually *done*. Merely to intend or will these things, to wish them or only think about them, is not sufficient. They must be done, and done perpetually:

> That charity and faith do not profit a man so long as they remain in only one part of his body, that is, in his head, and are not fixed in works, is evident from a thousand passages in the Word.
>
> From this it can be seen that charity and faith are not charity and faith until they exist in works, and that while they exist only in the expanse above works, that is, in the mind, they are like appearances of a tabernacle or temple in the air, which are nothing but a mirage, and vanish of themselves; or they are like pictures drawn on paper which moths consume; or they are like an abode on a housetop where there is no sleeping place, instead of in the house. All this shows that charity and faith are perishable things so long as they are merely mental or unless they are fixed in works and co-exist in them when possible" (*True Christian Religion* 376).

The internal and the external—the mind and the body—need to be working together.

The Motive

Finally, it is said that "these things should be done because they belong to God and are from God," and for no lesser reason. We are to do these good works for the glory of our Father in heaven (Matthew 5:16) because they belong to God and His kingdom wherever it is received.

If we do these good things for the Lord's sake (because He has commanded them in His Word), we are truly loving Him. For He said, "He who has My commandments and keeps them, he it is who loves Me" (John 14:21).

From that saying of the Lord, the supreme importance of theology is evident once more. In order to do good works for the Lord's sake and thus to love Him, we need to know who He is, what He is like, what He does, and so on. The answers to these questions constitute theology—wisdom about God.

Wisdom implies understanding. The concept of the Lord as a Divine Person makes it possible for us to think of Him, to think of His Divine qualities, and also to picture Him as a real and living Person. This causes Him to be present in our mind. Theology becomes not only understandable but also practical and useable.

Religion, then, is the application of theology to life. We are applying theology to life whenever we reflect that "evils should not be done because they belong to hell and are from hell" (thus against the Lord) and that "good things should be done because they belong to God and are from God." Both ethics and morality teach that good works ought to be done, and many of such works are identical to those we have been considering. However, unless theology enters into them, unless they are done *for* the Lord and *from* the Lord, they are dead works. There is no *spiritual* life or animation in them. They are done from the *natural* part of the mind only, the spiritual part of the mind being closed off.

That is why the Lord said: "Not everyone who says to Me, 'Lord, Lord,' shall enter the kingdom of heaven, but he who does the will of My Father in heaven. Many will say to Me in that day, 'Lord, Lord, have we not prophesied in Your name, cast out demons in Your name, and done many wonders in Your name?' And then I will declare to them, 'I never knew you; depart from Me, you who practice lawlessness'" (Matthew 7:21–23).

The great difference between spiritual life and mere morality is well brought out in the following passage from *The Apocalypse Explained* 182:1–2:

> Moral life is acting well, sincerely, and justly with one's companions in all the affairs and occupations of life; in a word, it is the life that is apparent before men, because it is the life lived with them. But this life has a two-fold origin; it is either from the love of self and the world, or it is from love to God and love towards the neighbor.

The passage goes on to explain that a moral life lived from love of self and the world is not really moral, although it seems moral. People living like that use morality, sincerity, and justice as means to attain their self-centered and worldly goals. They have to keep their real goals secret, because otherwise they would destroy the favorable image they have created, which is their means of achieving their goals. "Such a life," the passage concludes, "is merely craftiness and fraud."

Acknowledging that all good is from the Lord saves us from a host of evils. The first step in being delivered from evil is to recognize its source—that it flows into us from hell, from *outside* of us. Similarly, all goodness also flows in from outside of us, from the Lord—all the good motives of charity, mutual love, and goodwill from which alone genuinely good works can be done. Acknowledging that the Lord is the only source of goodness saves us from the illusion that we do what is good entirely from ourselves. Consequently, we will be saved from a sense of merit, from a desire for reward, from self-glory, self-praise, self-righteousness, self-worship. We will worship only the Lord, recognizing His "worth-ship"—the original meaning of the word *worship*. We will do good works *as if* of ourselves, but we will gladly realize that in reality we do them of and from the Lord.

12

"AS IF OF ONESELF"

These things should be done by man as if by himself; but it should be believed that they are from the Lord in man and by means of man.

Emanuel Swedenborg
True Christian Religion 3:2

A Problem Solved

Throughout the ages, there have been questions about such things as human free will, accountability, and the Lord's part in our preparation for heaven. At times, some have overemphasized the Lord's part to the point where human free will has entirely disappeared. An extreme case was Calvin's doctrine of predestination—that God decided arbitrarily who was to come into heaven and who was not. We could do nothing about it, either to save ourselves from hell or to prepare ourselves for heaven. If we were elected to heaven, nothing we did would keep us out of it. If we were assigned to hell, no action or belief on our part could change that.

Some, on the other hand, have exaggerated human free will to the point of leaving the Lord out of consideration altogether. The culmination of this attitude is mere humanism, "man the mighty."

Swedenborg's teaching—that we are to act *as if* of ourselves but acknowledge that it is really of and from the Lord that we do what is genuinely good—solves the problem. It includes human free will and action, but takes into account the reality rather than the appearance, the need for faith in the Lord. It reconciles charity and faith, and it unites them.

As a practical matter, what we have to do is this: we have to take the initiative *as if* the knowledge, the understanding, the belief, the desire, and the power to do what is good were in and from ourselves—*as if* there were no other power outside of ourselves. We have to act beforehand according to the appearance, but afterward—after having shunned what is evil or done what is good, after having rejected what is false and accepted what is true—we have to acknowledge from the heart that it was of and from the Lord that we did so. We have to do this on every particular occasion. That is the only way to come into a general acknowledgment and worship of the Lord in our life, for every general thing is made up of particular things. Every orchard is made up of particular trees. Without those particular trees, there would be no orchard.

Similarly, in the matter of acquiring a general and permanent acknowledgment, or *practical* worship of the Lord, we must acknowledge the Lord on particular occasions. This needs to be done every time we shun an evil as a sin against the Lord or do what is good from Him. We need to say to the Lord on particular occasions, "If that was really good, then it was from You, O Lord. For Yours is the kingdom, and the power, and the glory—forever."

Our natural mind loves the *first* part of Swedenborg's statement, that "these things should be done by man as if of himself." That seems to emphasize human independence. This can be overemphasized, however, so that we make a subtle change in our thought, changing "*as if* of oneself" to "*of* oneself." But our natural mind, while loving the first part of the statement, hates the *last* part: "but it should be believed that they are from the Lord in man and by means of man." We do not make that acknowledgment naturally; it does not come easily to us at first. But it simply must be made if we are to become spiritual and heavenly in quality.

The difficulty arises because "no man inherits a disposition to do [what is good and just] for the sake of what is good and just; consequently, only he who worships the Lord, and acts from Him when acting from himself, attains to spiritual charity, and becomes imbued with it by the practice of it," as we are told in *True Christian Religion* 423.

Let us look a little more closely at what a person does when acting "from [the Lord] when acting from himself," because this is the essence of the matter and is the same as saying that good works "should be done by man *as if by himself*; but it should be believed that they are from the Lord in man and by means of man."

The Basic Principle

Only the Lord lives in and from Himself. He alone is the source of His own life, for His life is life itself—the only life. This He Himself declared in the Gospel of John, when He said:

> "As the Father has life in Himself, so He has granted the Son to have life in Himself." (John 5:26)

> "I am the resurrection and the life." (John 11:25)

> "I am the way, the truth, and the life." (John 14:6)

But what is this Divine life? What is it that makes it to be what it is?

There are two things that make the Divine life: Divine love and Divine wisdom, which are the Divine warmth and the Divine light. The Lord is indeed the sun of the soul, the source of spiritual warmth (love) and spiritual light (wisdom). These together make Divine energy, or life.

The way the physical sun operates in this natural world is the same as the way the Lord operates on the spiritual plane. Just as the sun is the source of warmth, light, and physical energy, so the Lord is the source of love, wisdom, and life.

The Lord's life animates us; it flows forth from Him and is received into our souls. *To receive* means "to be acted upon." Plants are acted upon by the heat, light, and energy of the sun. Without this inflow, they would wither and die. So it is with us: without the inflow of life from the Lord into our soul moment by moment, we would cease to exist. We do indeed feel that we have life in ourselves, but it is really the Lord's life flowing in. "In Him [the Lord] we live and move and have our being" (Acts 17:28), or, as the same thought is expressed in Swedenborg's work *The Divine Providence* 46:3: "In a word, we are because God is."

We human beings, then, do not live from ourselves. We exist and subsist every moment from the Lord. He is our Creator every split second. A human being is an organ receiving life and being acted upon by it. A crude illustration of this would be the way an electric light bulb does not have light in itself; its light is produced by the electric current that flows into it from the power plant. The bulb is simply an organ receiving electricity. Similarly, a human being is an organ receiving life. We even read that there is nothing in a human being "except the state of receiving what flows in" (*The Apocalypse Revealed* 875).

The Image and Likeness

But human beings are made in the image of God and according to His likeness (Genesis 1:26). In other words, the goodness of the love flowing in from the Divine love itself acts upon the human mind—

specifically the human will—and produces a finite likeness of itself. This is what makes a person truly loving.

Now, the Divine love has three characteristics:

1. It wishes that there be others outside of Itself, who have nothing of Divinity or Infinity.

2. It wishes to be conjoined with those others, not be at odds with them or isolated from them.

3. It wishes to make them eternally happy or to give to others what is its own. (See *True Christian Religion* 43)

Consequently, when the human will in any person is touched or acted upon by the Divine love, that will becomes a finite likeness of the Divine love: it becomes aware of others outside of itself and of their needs; it longs to be joined with those others, rather than being isolated from them or at odds with them; it longs to make them happy not just temporarily but eternally, and it works for that goal; it longs to give what is its own to others. People whose will has been so acted upon are truly charitable people. Nor do they look for a reward for their good works, because they think of duty: "It becomes a citizen so to act," Swedenborg writes in *True Christian Religion* 423. Because it is their duty to do what is good, they feel no need for any reward or any feeling of having merited a reward. Their reward is in the doing (*The New Jerusalem and Its Heavenly Doctrine* 104). These genuinely good works are done simply "because they are of God and from God."

It is similar with human understanding. When acted upon by the Divine truth flowing forth from the Divine wisdom, the understanding becomes an image of the Divine wisdom. The term *likeness* refers to the will; the term *image* refers to the understanding or intellect. In a finite or limited way, the human understanding acted upon by the Divine wisdom produces ways and means of acting in conjunction with others outside of itself in order to make them happy to eternity, producing ways and means of giving what is its own to others.

Whereas life from the Lord flows in *directly* into the human soul, love and wisdom do *not* flow in directly. They come into the human mind indirectly, by the medium of the inhabitants of heaven. Nevertheless, love and wisdom are from the Lord; they originate in Him. The fact that the inhabitants of heaven act as agents in the transmission of Divine love and wisdom does not take away from the Divine origin of those qualities. We are therefore constantly reminded in the deeper view of Christianity that all good is from the Lord. That was indeed taught in earlier revelations of the Divine truth, especially in such statements as these in the New Testament:

"No one is good but One, that is, God." (Matthew 19:17)

"A man can receive nothing unless it has been given to him from heaven." (John 3:27)

Jesus said: "Abide in Me, and I in you. As the branch cannot bear fruit of itself unless it abides in the vine, neither can you unless you abide in Me. I am the vine, you are the branches. He who abides in Me, and I in him, bears much fruit; for without Me you can do nothing." (John 15:4–5. An alternative translation says, perhaps more graphically, ". . . severed from Me, you can do nothing.")

There is only one true altruist—the Lord Himself. The extent to which any human being is really altruistic is the extent to which he or she has been acted upon by the Lord. "With men this is impossible, but with God all things are possible" (Matthew 19:26).

There is actually a spiritual danger in denying or forgetting that all life flows in, and that the good we do is from the Lord and the evil we do is from hell. The teaching on this is painfully clear, that "everyone incurs guilt who believes that he acts from himself, whether it be good or whether it be evil" (*The Apocalypse Revealed* 224:9). But we are free to choose. In fact, we *are* what we choose.

The Source of Many Evils

The extremely serious consequences of identifying ourselves with the good feelings that flow in from the Lord are set out in the teaching that "without [acknowledging that all good is from the Lord] a person thinks the deeds he does earn him merit [a reward], and eventually righteousness; for to claim as one's own the truth and good that come from the Lord is self-righteousness. This is the source of many evils; for he then has himself in view in everything that he does for the neighbor, and when he does this, he loves himself above all others, whom he then despises if not in word, yet in heart" (*Arcana Coelestia* 5758).

Those "many evils" include not only a feeling of deserving a reward and self-righteousness, but also these:

- Contempt for others in comparison with oneself
- Confirming and consolidating self-centeredness
- Separating oneself from others
- Worrying about the future

The Lord's parable about the Pharisee's prayer in Luke 18 presents several examples of those evils: a sense of merit, self-righteousness, and contempt for others in comparison with oneself, not to mention separating oneself from "the weaker brethren" in that "the Pharisee stood and prayed . . . with himself" (Luke 18:11).

The divisive separation and disunity (together with a growing love of self) that result from self-righteousness is further discussed in this passage from *Arcana Coelestia* 2027:

Those who place merit in the actions of their lives do not have charity's faith . . . for in doing this they wish to be saved, not because of the Lord's righteousness, but because of their own. . . . No faith belonging to charity is in them, that is, no charity. This is evident from the fact that they put themselves before other people, and so have themselves in view and not other people, except insofar as the latter serve them; and they either despise or hate those who are unwilling to serve them. Thus by self-love they disassociate, and never associate, and in this way destroy what is heavenly, namely, mutual love, which gives heaven its stability. . . . This is the nature of people who place merit in the actions of their lives and claim righteousness for themselves.

The same spiritually dangerous attitude is also illustrated in the Gospels by the well-known incident when the Lord was invited into the home of the two sisters, Martha and Mary:

> Now it happened as they went, that He entered a certain village; and a certain woman named Martha welcomed Him into her house. And she had a sister called Mary, who also sat at Jesus' feet and heard His word. But Martha was distracted with much serving, and approached Him, and said, "Lord, do You not care that my sister has left me to serve alone? Therefore tell her to help me." And Jesus answered and said to her, "Martha, Martha, you are worried and troubled about many things. But one thing is needed, and Mary has chosen that good part, which will not be taken away from her." (Luke 10:38–42)

Mary, who "sat at Jesus' feet and heard His word," represents those who act from *spiritual* motives, from a spiritual kind of hearkening or obedience to the Lord's Word. But Martha, being "distracted with much serving," represents those who think that they do what is good from themselves, that there is no other source of goodness, that they must "serve alone." They are therefore contemptuous of others, thinking that they are doing more than anyone else, making invidious comparisons between themselves and others who seem to be doing less than they are doing. They even incline to rebuke the Lord for not compelling others to help them. Bearing in mind these consequences of self-righteousness, we can understand why the Lord rebuked Martha for being "worried and troubled about many things," while praising Mary for having "chosen that good part," which He promised would not be taken away from her.

Worry is another inevitable consequence of trying to do good from ourselves and not from the Lord. The reason is that, with the Lord effectively blotted out from our thought, we feel—

consciously or unconsciously—that we have to do it all, that there is no one else. With regard to our preparation for heaven, if we act as if we have to do it all, we are like the people in the book of Genesis who tried to climb up to heaven by their own efforts, by building the tower of Babel (Genesis 11:4). The Lord must continually counter this attitude. He must work against it to bring us to our knees, so to speak. We must come finally to realize that "with men this is impossible, but with God all things are possible" (Matthew 19:26). Until we reach that point, we will be more or less plagued with worry—"care for the morrow."

> People have care for the morrow when they are not content with their lot, do not trust in God but in themselves, and have in view only worldly and earthly things, and not heavenly things. People like that are ruled completely by anxiety about the future, and desire to possess all things, and dominate over everyone. That desire is kindled and grows greater and greater, and finally does so beyond all measure. They grieve if they do not obtain the objects of their desire, and are anguished at the loss of them. They have no consolation because of the anger they feel against the Divine, which they reject—together with everything of faith—and curse themselves. Such are those who have care for the morrow. (*Arcana Coelestia* 8478:2)

That passage appears in the explanation of the words in Genesis: "And Moses said, 'Let no one leave any of it [the manna] till morning'" (Exodus 16:19). The Lord had provided manna for the Israelites in the wilderness when they were starving. He provided enough for each day, so they were forbidden to store up any residue for the next day. If they did so, what would that mean? What attitude would it reveal?

It would show that they did not really trust the Lord to provide what was needed day by day, that they trusted only themselves, that they felt *they* had better make provision in case the Lord failed to provide.

How true the teaching is that doing good from ourselves is "the source of many evils" (*Arcana Coelestia* 5758)! To avoid all this misery, we need to recall the truth—the reality—that all good is from the Lord, and that consequently any genuinely good works we do—anything that springs from real goodwill or genuine charity—is from the Lord in us, and that to Him belong the kingdom, the power, and the glory. This obviously leads to true worship of the Lord and heartfelt thanksgiving. We cannot be truly humble before the Lord and receive the blessings that He wishes to give us unless we make the acknowledgment that all genuinely good deeds are "of God and from God," and that, when doing a genuinely good deed, we are acting from the Lord while acting from ourselves.

Why the Appearance?

Despite the fact that we cannot really do good deeds from ourselves alone, it must *appear* to us that we do these things of and from ourselves. Why must this be so?

If we had no other feeling than that the Divine power was pushing us into action, if we felt that we could do nothing by or from ourselves, we would not be human beings. We would be like soulless machines. We would have no freedom of choice.

But the Lord gives us not only life but also freedom of choice and reason—the faculty of making our choice between what is from Him and what is from hell, together with the faculty of having a rational view of life as set forth in the Divine Word.

The truth that we have freedom of choice is clear from many passages in the Word of God, but especially from this one in Deuteronomy 30:15–19:

> See, I have set before you this day life and good, death and evil, in
> that I command you today to love the Lord your God, to walk in
> His ways, and to keep His commandments and His statutes and
> His judgments, that you may live and multiply; and the Lord your

God will bless you in the land which you go to possess. But if your heart turns away so that you do not hear but are drawn away, and worship other gods and serve them, I announce to you today that you shall surely perish; you shall not prolong your days in the land which you cross over the Jordan to go and possess. I call heaven and earth as witnesses today against you, that I have set before you life and death, blessing and cursing; therefore choose life, that both you and your descendants may live.

This faculty of freedom does not belong to any human being, but is the Lord's with us. Yet the faculties of freedom and reason are what make us to be human beings; without those faculties we would be like animals, which have neither of these two faculties, and consequently are not free but are ruled by a general inflow of life. They do not have to choose between what is of order and what is not, for the simple reason that it is impossible for them to go outside the order of life that belongs to their genera and species. Only with human beings is this possible; it is possible only with us to depart from the order of life Divinely appointed for us: that we should love the Lord above all else and our neighbor as ourselves. Only humans can be diverted and perverted from their true order. This is one of the consequences of our being granted freedom of choice, but who among us would have it otherwise?

Together with the faculty of freedom of choice, the Lord also gives us the faculty of reason, which animals also do not have. Their mental life is limited to finding ways and means to follow their instincts. The ratio between the eternal and the temporal—between the spiritual and the natural—is a concept that is quite beyond them. Only human beings can reason in this sense; only humans can see the *ratio* between life to eternity and life in this world of time and space, and thus evaluate the spiritual and the natural. Only humans can be truly *ratio*-nal.

The Lord gives us human beings these two faculties precisely so that we may act in freedom according to what seems to us to be reason, and consequently act to all appearances *as if* of ourselves. He allows us to have a certain determination of our life.

Without this ability to act *as if* of ourselves (yet really from the faculties given to us by the Lord), we could not be an image and likeness of God. He acts *of* Himself and *from* Himself. We *appear* to act of and from ourselves. Unless it so appeared to us, we could make no response to the inflowing life from the Lord, nor could we make any response to the inflowing love and wisdom that perpetually go forth from Him. There would be no reception and no reciprocation of His love and wisdom. Freedom of choice is acted out in our *mind*.

Without reciprocating or responding to what flows in from the Lord, we could not be conjoined with Him. Because God is love itself, He wishes to create others outside of Himself and to be conjoined with those others for the sake of making them eternally happy. God could not do this unless we reciprocated, unless we responded to the Divine action or life. Reception and reciprocation on our part are absolutely essential. As we read in the *Doctrine of Life* 102:

> To love and to be conjoined with one in whom there is nothing reciprocal is not possible, nor is it possible to enter in and abide with one in whom there is no reception. As there are in man, from the Lord, reception and reciprocation, the Lord says: "He who has My commandments and does them, he it is who loves Me. . . . And I will love him, and will abide with him" (John 14:21–23). So the Lord dwells in man in what is His own, and the man dwells in those things that are from the Lord, and in this way he dwells in the Lord.

Swedenborg's work *The Divine Providence* appeals to reason to confirm the truth that there must be reception and reciprocation on our part:

> Anyone can see from reason alone that there is no conjunction of minds unless it is reciprocal, and that the reciprocation is what conjoins. If one loves another and is not loved in return, then as

one approaches, the other withdraws; but if he is loved in return, and as one approaches, the other approaches, then conjunction does take place. Moreover, love wills to be loved; this is implanted in it; and so far as love is loved in return, it is in itself and in its enjoyment. This makes clear that when the Lord loves man and is not loved in return by man, the Lord approaches and man withdraws (*The Divine Providence* 92:2).

Because we have this ability to reciprocate, the Lord can command us to keep His commandments and perform the work of repentance. If we could not act *as if* of ourselves, it would make no sense at all for the Lord to exhort us to choose life rather than spiritual death, to do good and depart from evil, or for Him to say such things as, "Unless you repent you will all . . . perish" (Luke 13:3, 5), and "Why do you call Me 'Lord, Lord,' and not do the things that I say?" (Luke 6:46)

Unless we appeared to live and act *as if* from ourselves, the life that flows in from the Lord would have no receptacle; it would simply flow through unreceived. We could not even live unless it appeared to us that we live of and from ourselves.

Similarly, in order for our minds to be acted upon by the Divine love and the Divine wisdom, we have to respond to them and reciprocate them. We have to act and think as if of ourselves. If we were to hang down our hands and wait for some inflow of love and of thought from the Lord, we would stay like that to eternity. We would be nothing more than statues. As we read in the *Arcana Coelestia* 1712:3:

> The Lord cannot flow into anyone who deprives himself of everything that power can be poured into. It is as if one were not willing to learn anything without a revelation to himself; or as if one were unwilling to teach anything unless the words were put into him; or as if one would not attempt anything unless he were put into action like someone without a will. . . . So it is an eternal truth that a person does not live from himself, but that if he did not appear to do so, he could not live at all.

Without the appearance that we act and think of and from ourselves, we would have no sense of individuality, no feelings of achievement, no joy from being useful, none of the delight of usefulness that makes heaven so everlastingly happy.

Scripture Illustrations

This ability to act "as if of oneself" but really from the Lord is very graphically brought out in the Old Testament Word, especially in the story of the fortunes of the Israelites. Whenever they went into a battle trusting in their own strength alone, they were always miserably and abjectly defeated. But when they looked to the Lord and believed that He went with them into the battle, that they were acting from Him as they acted from themselves, then they were always victorious and attributed the victory to the Lord, making a thank-offering to Him afterward.

The same is true of our personal temptation battles. When we attempt to fight the hells from ourselves—when we hope that Satan will cast out Satan—we are miserably unsuccessful and in danger of being overwhelmed by hopelessness. But if we shun our evils as sins *as if* of ourselves, believing that this repudiation is really from the Lord in us, He can then work to remove our deep-seated craving for those evils (*The Divine Providence* 100, 120). The Lord can operate only as we cooperate. We have to act from the Lord when acting from ourselves.

Two stories in particular teach this truth: the conquest of the city of Jericho and the defeat at Ai (Joshua 6–8). All that the Israelites had to do at Jericho was to obey explicitly the Lord's instructions. He had expressly commanded Joshua to take Jericho, promising that He would give it into his hands. The Israelites, therefore, had full confidence that He was with them in the battle. But they did have to act *as if* of themselves. They had to compel themselves to carry out the Lord's instructions in detail. They needed trumpeters to blow the trumpets, men who had the confidence and skill to do so. They did not wait for an influx of power from the Lord to move them into action. They acted as if of themselves.

Yet they did acknowledge that they were acting of and from the Lord, that the plan was His, and that He was indeed the victor. Accordingly, after the battle, all the spoils of war (the silver, gold, and vessels of brass and iron) were consecrated to the Lord. The people were not to take away any of the spoils of war for themselves, but were to acknowledge that they belonged "in the treasury of the Lord" (Joshua 6:19).

In a very different manner, the Israelites' first attempt to take the city of Ai immediately after the victory at Jericho was pathetically unsuccessful, representing what happens to us spiritually when we fail to call on the Lord, but act according to the appearance rather than the reality. We steal from the Lord. This was the sin of Achan, who stole the "accursed things" (Joshua 7:1). We profane what is good and true when we attribute them to ourselves. This profanation is represented by Achan, who had to be completely destroyed.

Note that Joshua was not commanded by the *Lord* to take Ai. That was his own idea. There was likewise something egotistical in the contemptuous report of the men whom he had sent to survey the city. On their return, they boastfully predicted an easy victory over the men of Ai. Their overconfidence on the natural plane is equivalent to self-confidence in spiritual things.

When at Ai, the Israelites were miserably defeated and humbled. Joshua fell on his knees before the Lord, imploring His help as his men fled before the men of Ai. The task of conquering the *whole* land must have seemed completely hopeless if the performance at Ai were to become the pattern of the future (see Joshua 7).

The land of Canaan represents heaven. Entering into the land means entering into heaven. The conquest of the various cities in the land pictures our conquest (as if of ourselves) of the various evils and falsities that stand as obstacles. If we rely on self in our spiritual life and in our preparation for heaven, we will suffer the same abject failure that befell the Israelites when they attempted to take Ai *of themselves.* But if we fall on our knees before the Lord, imploring His help, acknowledging that without it we can do nothing—if we cast out the conceit that the good we do and the truth we believe from the Lord are actually ours—then the Lord will reveal to us the proper strategy for spiritual success, just as He revealed to Joshua the strategy for successfully taking Ai on the second attempt.

Spiritually, all we have to do then is to follow the Lord's revealed plan completely and willingly, knowing that He will grant the victory. The Lord can operate only so far as we cooperate.

Very significantly, after the successful capture of Ai, "Joshua built an altar to the Lord God of Israel in Mount Ebal, as Moses the servant of the Lord commanded the Children of Israel, as it is written in the Book of the Law of Moses, 'an altar of whole stones over which no man has wielded an iron tool.' And they offered on it burnt offerings to the Lord, and sacrificed peace offerings" (Joshua 8:30–31).

Summary of Part Two

In the work *True Christian Religion*, where the "particulars of faith on man's part" are set forth, the first two are called matters of faith (belief). These are:

God is one, in whom is a Divine trinity, and the Lord God the Savior Jesus Christ is that one.

Saving faith is to believe in *Him.*

The next two are called matters of charity. These are:

Evils should not be done, because they belong to the devil and are from the devil.

Good things should be done, because they belong to God and are from God.

The fifth particular, about acting "as if of oneself," is called a matter of "conjoining charity and faith, thus of the conjunction of the Lord and man" (*True Christian Religion* 3). To shun evils as sins against the Lord and as a consequence to do good things from Him—*as if* from ourselves—is a matter of charity.

But it is a matter of enlightened, saving faith to believe the truth and not the appearance, the truth being that these things are from the Lord in us and by means of us, that the power, the inclination, and the wisdom to do these things are of and from the Lord and from Him alone.

So the faith of the New Christianity begins with the *faithful* acknowledgment of the Lord Jesus Christ, that He is the one and only God. But it ends with the *practical* acknowledgment of Him in our daily lives. In the deeper view of Christianity, the Lord Jesus Christ is to be worshiped not only intellectually but practically, in every part of our daily lives.

APPENDIX: THE DEVIL

Traditionally, the devil has been regarded as a person—usually called Satan. This belief is confirmed by the account in the Gospels of the Lord's temptations, when He went into the wilderness for forty days and was tempted of the devil, who seems to be just one person. In the Gospel of Mark 1:13, it is said that the Lord was tempted "by Satan."

In some parts of the Christian Church, there has also sprung up a belief that this person called "the devil" is "a fallen angel." The reference usually quoted in support of this is Isaiah 14:12:

> How are you fallen from heaven, O Lucifer, son of the morning!
> How are you cut down to the ground, you who did weaken the nations!

That verse, *if wrested from its context*, could give the impression that Lucifer was someone who had fallen from heaven.

But how this could happen is never explained. However, when we set this verse in its context, a very different picture emerges. Historically viewed, Isaiah 14 foretells Israel's triumph over Babylon. Specifically, verse 4 gives a warning to the king of Babylon: "You will take up this proverb against the king of Babylon, and say: 'How the oppressor has ceased, the golden city ceased!' Although a prophecy of the future, it is written as though the defeat had already taken place. This mode of writing is very common in the Old Testament.

In verse 12, the king of Babylon is called "Lucifer, son of the morning." The name Lucifer means "shining one." This, coupled with the words "son of the morning", obviously refers to the splendor and glory of the Babylonian empire with its insatiable ambition to dominate. Verses 13 and 14 make this abundantly clear, for the king of Babylon is quoted as saying, "I will ascend into heaven, . . . I will ascend above the heights of the clouds, I will be like the Most High."

The "Lucifer" described here is not "the devil", nor was he ever in heaven itself! He only dreamed of ascending to heaven. The "heaven" from which Lucifer, the shining one, is said to have fallen is only an imaginary one—a "heaven" of his imagination. The passage does not say that he was actually in heaven. How could he be there when he was reigning over the Babylonian empire on earth?

The foundations for the notion that the devil is a fallen angel are really quite fragile. If we go beyond the literal sense to the spiritual meaning of this chapter, we can readily see that the subject is the fall of what is represented by Babylon (or Babel)—namely, the love of dominion, the love of ruling even over spiritual things and over heaven itself. The next few verses reveal the spiritual meaning of this chapter: "For you have said in your heart: 'I will ascend into heaven, I will exalt my throne above the stars of God; I will also sit on the mount of the congregation on the farthest sides of the north; I will ascend above the height of the clouds, I will be like the Most High.' Yet you shall be brought down to Sheol, to the lowest depths of the Pit" (Isa. 14:13–15).

Another passage sometimes quoted in support of the idea that the devil is a fallen angel is in the Gospel of Luke 10:18:

And (the Lord) said to them, I beheld Satan fall like lightning from heaven.

Again, the general context shows how this is to be understood. The Lord had sent out the disciples to preach the Gospel. They had returned rejoicing, saying, "Lord, even the demons are subject to us through Your name" (verse 17). The Lord's response about Satan's fall follows. The real heaven cannot be meant, for the Lord Himself pointed out in Luke 16 that there is a great gulf fixed between heaven and hell, so that those who wish to pass from heaven to hell cannot, neither can those come into heaven who would like to come out of hell (see Luke 16:26). That verse states a universal law admitting of no exceptions. The Lord was surely speaking figuratively to the disciples, confirming their observation that they had power over even the devils when they acted in His name. In verse 18, He was referring to casting out the devils from the "imaginary heavens" that had formed in the world of spirits.

Verse 15 reads: "And you, Capernaum, who are *exalted to heaven*, shall be thrust down to hell." Are we to suppose that the inhabitants of Capernaum here referred to are all "fallen angels" merely because Capernaum is said to be "exalted to heaven"? The inhabitants of Capernaum, living in this world, had never been to heaven, any more than Lucifer, king of Babylon had. The meaning is that Capernaum had exalted itself "to the sky," an equally faithful translation of the original Greek.

We conclude, then, that there is no basis either in Scripture or in common sense for the idea that the devil is a fallen angel.

The idea that Satan is only one person was examined in chapter 10.

BIBLIOGRAPHY OF WORKS BY EMANUEL SWEDENBORG

Apocalypse Explained. 6 vols. Translated by John Whitehead. 2nd ed. West Chester, Penna: The Swedenborg Foundation, 1994–1998.

Apocalypse Revealed. 2 vols. Translated by John Whitehead. 2nd ed. West Chester, Penna: The Swedenborg Foundation, 1997.

Arcana Coelestia. 12 vols. Translated by John Clowes. Revised by John F. Potts. 2nd ed. West Chester, Penna: The Swedenborg Foundation, 1995–1998. The first volume of this work is also available under the title *Heavenly Secrets.*

Charity: The Practice of Neighborliness. Translated by William F. Wunsch. Edited by William R. Woofenden. West Chester, Penna: The Swedenborg Foundation, 1995.

Conjugial Love. Translated by Samuel S. Warren. Revised by Louis Tafel. 2nd ed. West Chester, Penna: The Swedenborg Foundation, 1998. This volume is also available under the title *Love in Marriage,* translated by David Gladish, 1992.

Divine Love and Wisdom. Translated by John C. Ager. 2nd ed. West Chester, Penna: The Swedenborg Foundation, 1995. This volume is also available in a translation by George F. Dole.

Divine Providence. Translated by William Wunsch. 2nd ed. West Chester, Penna: The Swedenborg Foundation, 1996.

Four Doctrines. Translated by John F. Potts. 2nd ed. West Chester, Penna: The Swedenborg Foundation, 1997.

Heaven and Hell. Translated by John C. Ager. 2nd ed. West Chester, Penna: The Swedenborg Foundation, 1995. This volume is also available in a translation by George F. Dole.

The Heavenly City. Translated by Lee Woofenden. West Chester, Penna: The Swedenborg Foundation, 1993.

Journal of Dreams. Translated by J. J. G. Wilkinson. Introduction by Wilson Van Dusen. New York: The Swedenborg Foundation, 1986.

The Last Judgment in Retrospect. Translated by and edited by George F. Dole. West Chester, Penna: The Swedenborg Foundation, 1996.

Miscellaneous Theological Works. Translated by John Whitehead. 2nd ed. West Chester, Penna: The Swedenborg Foundation, 1996. This volume includes *The New Jerusalem and Its Heavenly Doctrine, Earths in the Universe,* and *The Last Judgment and Babylon Destroyed,* among others.

Posthumous Theological Works. 2 vols. Translated by John Whitehead. 2nd ed. West Chester, Penna: The Swedenborg Foundation, 1996. These volumes include the autobiographical and theological extracts from Swedenborg's letters, additions to *True Christian Religion, The Doctrine of Charity, The Precepts of the Decalogue,* and collected minor works, among others.

True Christian Religion. 2 vols. Translated by John C. Ager. West Chester, Penna: The Swedenborg Foundation, 1996.

Worship and Love of God. Translated by Alfred H. Stroh and Frank Sewall. 2nd ed. West Chester, Penna: The Swedenborg Foundation, 1996.

Collections of Swedenborg's Writings

Conversations with Angels: What Swedenborg Heard in Heaven. Edited by Leonard Fox and Donald Rose. Translated by David Gladish and Jonathan Rose. West Chester, Penna: Chrysalis Books, 1996.

Debates with Devils: What Swedenborg Heard in Hell. Edited by Donald Rose. Translated by Lisa Hyatt Cooper. West Chester, Penna: Chrysalis Books, 2000.

A Thoughtful Soul. Translated by and edited by George F. Dole. West Chester, Penna: Chrysalis Books, 1995.

Way of Wisdom: Meditations on Love and Service. Edited by Grant R. Schnarr and Erik J. Buss. West Chester, Penna: Chrysalis Books, 1999.